ADVANCE PRAISE FOR
Surrounded by Love

A beautiful meditation on the spiritual wisdom of the Povercllo and its practical value for today. In this elegantly written book, Murray Bodo brings Francis of Assisi's life experiences and teachings into dialogue with our contemporary world, showing our need for the breathtaking beauty of the Franciscan spiritual and theological visions.
—MARY BETH INGHAM, CSJ, Franciscan School of Theology

Fr. Murray Bodo illuminates the grace of the Franciscan tradition and its ongoing relevance, importance, and timeliness with each of his brilliant and poetic books. Surrounded by Love is both an introduction to and a meditation on the wisdom of St. Francis of Assisi that the world so desperately needs today. This is a must-read book!
—DANIEL P. HORAN, OFM, author, *God is Not Fair and other Reasons for Gratitude* and *Dating God: Live and Love in the Way of St. Francis.*

Whether you are new to the Franciscan tradition or deeply rooted in its spirituality, *Surrounded by Love* is a wonderfully inspiring read. While the stories of St. Francis may be familiar to many, Murray Bodo's storytelling ability and poetic insights give them a renewed character, allowing the reader to enter into the mind and heart of the great saint in a profound way.
—CASEY COLE, OFM, founder of Breaking in the Habit Media and author of *Called: What Happens After Saying Yes to God*

Fr. Murray Bodo has lost nothing of the joy, freshness and vitality that characterized his writing when he was a newly vowed young friar. Yet, his latest work, *Surrounded by Love: Seven Teachings from Saint Francis,* possesses something else: wisdom. It is a gift received after a lifetime spent serving others: as friar and priest, as pilgrimage leader, as teacher and mentor, as companion to the countless friends he has made around the world. What emerges here are seven teachings passed on to Fr. Murray through close and intimate relationship not only with St. Francis of Assisi, but with Jesus Christ himself. Thank you, Fr. Murray, for the gift of this newest book.

—BRET THOMAN, OFS, author of *St. Francis of Assisi: Passion, Poverty, and the Man Who Transformed the Catholic Church* and *St Clare of Assisi: Light from the Cloister*

To live a Franciscan life, we must live the Gospel and embrace its basic truth. Murray Bodo clearly and poetically expresses how the Franciscan life is to be lived in this seven-part outline of the way St. Francis of Assisi embraced the Gospel life, underscoring each essential principle with quotes from early Franciscan works.

—BARB SZYSZKIEWICZ, OFS, editor of CatholicMom.com and managing editor of *Today's Catholic Teacher*

Surrounded by Love

Seven Teachings from Saint Francis

Murray Bodo, OFM

franciscan
media
Cincinnati, Ohio

Cover and book design by Mark Sullivan

Copyright ©2018, Murray Bodo, OFM

ISBN 978-1-63253-237-4

Published by Franciscan Media
28 W. Liberty St.
Cincinnati, OH 45202
www.FranciscanMedia.org

Printed in the United States of America.
Printed on acid-free paper.
18 19 20 21 22   5 4 3 2 1

CONTENTS

ACKNOWLEDGMENTS

I WANT TO GRATEFULLY ACKNOWLEDGE THE VALUABLE suggestions of my readers, Judith Emery, Susan Saint Sing, John Feister, and Episcopal Franciscan Tertiary, Brother Willy. In addition I want to thank the organizers of the Episcopal Third Order's 100th Anniversary of the Convocation of the Americas for asking me to deliver the keynote address out of which this book grew. And finally, I want to thank Diane M. Houdek, my editor at Franciscan Media, and all the others involved in bringing this book to print, especially Mark Sullivan for the design and cover of this and other books I've written over the years.

ONCE, NEARLY EIGHT DECADES AGO NOW, WHEN I felt lost and
confused in my burgeoning adolescence, Jesus gave me St.
Francis as my brother and friend, and I began to trade my own
self-absorption for the adventure of the Holy Quest: the ascent
of Mount Subasio on whose eastern side Francis was born and
lived his youth in the armed and walled city of Assisi. What I
mistook for an immediate ascent of that holy mountain began
first with a descent from the high city of Assisi to the plain below
where the lepers lived. That metaphor meant that I had to learn
the hard way that we have to live in the real world among those
who, at times, are not easy to live with at first, but who teach us
what loving is really about.

We have to learn that living on the mountain top of spiritual
experiences is an ideal, a dream, and only by first learning to live
in peace with those who don't have the same ideals or who differ
from us in other ways, can we hope to ascend the mountain of
union with God. That's what Francis had to do before he could
ascend the mystical mountain of La Verna in a wooded area of
Tuscany where he received the sacred stigmata of Christ. And
that's what Jesus did when he first descended from heaven to
live among us and then ascended into heaven from the Mount
of Olives. That going down in order to ascend is what I have
learned from St. Francis from the time I left home at an early age

to follow in the footsteps of this extraordinary man who walked in the footsteps of Jesus until now so many years after. I put this journey with Francis into a poem, years after I began the journey into God with him.

FRANCIS SHOWS HOW WE OPEN HEAVEN

When I was a boy, I thought that heaven
Must start behind the stars, their lights
Holes in night that covered God like curtains.
There had to be a secret cord that drew them,
Revealing God's apartments. Saint Francis
Said an enemy's hand was creased with
Codes that told the merest boy how to
Open God's bright heaven. The hidden
Handle was the enemy's very hand, and
Hateful eyes were openings to glory. But
How was I to know what lightless labyrinths
Those creases trace, how long it takes to
Travel easy there before the handle turns?[1]

And now, almost seventy years after I began this Quest to rise by going down, I have come to a further understanding of what I have learned from Francis. And as I began to write, his teachings naturally emerged as seven in number, a mystical number of perfection, having all the religious resonance of the seven days of creation and the seven days of re-creation as when Noah sends out a dove from the ark, but it returns having found no dry land to rest upon. He then sends the dove out again; and after seven days the dove returns with a freshly plucked olive leaf in its beak, a sign that the waters that had covered the earth had receded, and the earth will be renewed.

In the medieval times of St. Francis, the number seven held a sacred, mystical power, as in the seven cardinal virtues, the seven deadly sins, and, most importantly, the seven sacraments. And in the high point of medieval literature, Dante's *Divine Comedy*, there is the seven-storey mountain of purgatory which the imperfect must climb to be purified of the effects of sin and guilt before they can enter paradise. Dante himself could not make that ascent until he had first descended into hell.

It is not surprising then, that these teachings of St. Francis are seven in number and flow one from another, and all together they outline a spirituality for our own time that anyone can learn to practice in his or her own life, anyone who has an attitude of reverence for others and for Earth and all of nature, and who acknowledges the existence of a higher power that is beyond what one can perceive with the senses. These seven teachings are both a way and a destination, the way being transformation and the destination being the love of God. It is a drama that ends up being a comedy in the sense that *The Divine Comedy* is a comedy, namely, a story with a happy ending that is union with God for those who make the journey that God has mapped out for us in our creation and transformation into the redeemed child of God we were created to become. It is a journey from love through love into love.

IT WAS THE VERY CLOSENESS OF GOD that moved him to the depths of his being. He was no longer alone. God was with him and with the whole world. God was in him and God was in every creature, and all was blessing.

His name was Francis, the son of Pietro Bernardone, a cloth-merchant, and Lady Pica, his mother, who was of French origin, and they lived in Assisi, Italy in the late twelfth and early thirteenth century. He was a man born of wealth, a leader who dreamed of knighthood and who went to war on a high steed only to be brought low to the earth in defeat and imprisonment that marked him with what has been the fate of countless soldiers and prisoners of war throughout the centuries. Some say that mark was what today we call post-traumatic stress, an experience that affected Francis his whole life long until, singing "Bring me out of prison," the words of Psalm 142, David's prayer in a cave, he entered eternity on the high steed of evangelical poverty and intimate union with Jesus Christ, his Lord and Savior.

It was that very Jesus who became for him, and all his followers, the closeness of God. For Jesus was and is the closeness of God. He is God become one of us, like us in everything but sin. He is the mystery of the incarnation of God, and that mystery was deepened for Francis with the knowledge that this Incarnate

God can become present in us through the sacramental grace of the mystery of the Holy Eucharist wherein we eat the body and drink the blood of Christ whose effect is to intensify the indwelling of God in us.

St. Francis was not a medieval theologian, but a wisdom figure, a teacher of wisdom who used sayings, stories, and rituals to show us how we can allow God to transform our lives. In this, as in everything else, he was following in the footsteps of Jesus, who is the mystery of the fullness of God among us.

The Wonder of the Incarnation is the first and central teaching that St. Francis left us. And from that core teaching six other teachings cascade: *The Paradox of Evangelical Poverty* and how it unites us to God and leads to *Living the Gospel* in our time and place. This living the Gospel leads to how we are to *Go and Repair God's House*, and we repair God's house by *Making Peace*. Peacemaking leads to the realization that *God's House is All of Creation*. These first six teachings all involve a going down in order to rise. Then, in the fullness of time, our living of these teachings are brought to completion in *The Joy of Humble Praise and Service of God* by embracing and serving all of God's creatures. This joy, then, accompanies our final rising in a symbolic return to paradise. All seven teachings are rooted in the love of God, and so I have added an eighth chapter, entitled *The Teaching of Teachings: Love*.

This simple map for living is why St. Francis is still listened to and followed today in our fractious and divided world. What he teaches, if lived out, brings joy, which is the result of union with God who lives with us and within all of creation. God lives in creation but is also apart from creation as its Creator who existed before the existence of the universe.

St. Francis's teachings, then, become both a theology and a way of living. They are a theology that emerges from the concrete, practical choices he made in the effort to follow in the footsteps of Jesus, who is *the* teacher and the embodiment of what it means to live and love in God.

As St. John says in his First Letter, "As for you, the anointing that you received from him abides in you, and so you do not need anyone to teach you. But as his anointing teaches you about all things, and is true and is not a lie, and just as it has taught you, abide in him." (1 John 2:27).

This Christ, this anointing, is what the teaching of St. Francis is about. Christ *is* the revelation of God. In a sermon on the Feast of St. Francis in 1255 St. Bonaventure said of his holy father Francis that he was a true teacher because he learned the truth of God's revelation, gave his whole heart to what was being taught by Christ, and did not forget what he'd been taught because he put what he learned into practice. So, in the end, Francis's teachings are concretized and made visible in his choices and in his practices, which are the result of hearing and living the truth given him by Christ.

This book attempts to explore these experiences and these choices of St. Francis and show how they resulted in lessons that when we act upon them today, continue to unfold as counter valences to the negative, immature "acting out" that has led and continues to lead to the divisions and hatreds that split us apart. The teachings of St. Francis enable us to imagine another future that gives us hope; for hope is the grace to imagine a future more positive, more loving, and more joyful than the world we now find ourselves in. As St. Francis used to say to his brothers, "Let us begin to do good, for up to now we have done nothing."

FIRST TEACHING

Jesus Christ is the Fullness of the Incarnation of God

HIS FATHER PIETRO WAS AWAY FOR MANY months at a time when Francis was a boy. He would be in France buying cloth, and Francis would wait. He would go out to the city gate of San Giacomo and play with his friends there. But that was only a ruse. He was really there in that quarter of the city hoping he would see his father and his retinue riding toward Assisi, the mules loaded down with bolts of cloth. The waiting was long but he had learned to wait because his father would always return.

But this was different. He was in prison, a dungeon deep inside a cliff of rock in Perugia. He'd been here for months. He kept waiting while he worked like a slave hauling stones. But his father never came. Day after day after day. The seasons had changed twice before he realized he was no longer waiting. Something had happened to him. He knew his father would not come. Like God, his father had abandoned him to his own fate.

He began to have nightmares, and in the dreams he would be playing outside the Porta San Giacomo in Assisi, waiting for his father. Then suddenly he would see him in the distance, and he would begin to wave and yell, "Papa, Papa," and the keepers of the gate would start to open the great wooden doors, and Francis would be jumping for joy hardly able to restrain himself from squeezing through the opening when it was just beginning to slowly inch open. And then he would finally fit into the opening in the doors, and he'd wiggle through with the gate keepers laughing and threatening him, saying they were going to drop the portcullis on him. But he would break free just in time, and begin running toward the horses and the men hailing him, and then he would speed up in one final burst of energy reaching out to a sudden awakening: he was screaming in the dark of the prison, his friends trying to calm him. "Calma, Francesco, it's okay; it is only a dream!" And he would then slump back against the cold stone, knowing he was still trapped. There was no way out.

And so they began, the terrible nights: the shaking, the need to keep his back to the wall so he could see whoever might be advancing toward him to harm him. He became obsessively on his guard. He was no longer safe. God and his father no longer existed. At least they did not exist for him. They were distance, indifference, dismissal. He was alone, though his fellow prisoners were all around him. When would they, too, turn away or, worse, turn on him? He had to be vigilant day and night.

His only consolation was to retreat into reverie and connect to his former passion for knighthood. He would picture himself victorious, the great knight he would have become had he not been captured and put in prison. He had to keep alive the knightly ideal and code. He began to live in his mind and imagination. His imagination would show him how not to be defeated by giving him hope that all of this would change. He could see it in

his mind's eye. And this made him joyful. He began to encourage
his fellow prisoners. He had hope again because he could once
more imagine that someday there would be a castle, a lady, a
Round Table. King Arthur would find him and Arthur would
replace his father and his absent God.

This imagined scene from Francis's time in prison sets the
scene for his first teaching, namely, that the seemingly absent
Father-God sent his son to live among us to be the tangible presence of God, a God who could be imagined because he was a
human being like us, and his name was Jesus and he lived in
Palestine over a thousand years before Francis was born. And
Francis met him when he most needed to know God's presence
to him, to know God's face. And it all happened when he was
finally released from prison in Perugia and returned to Assisi a
broken man. Let us imagine that scene:

And then he was released and told he was free; he could go
home. He stood there motionless, the Umbrian sun blinding and
hurting his eyes, which had become accustomed to darkness. He
took a few halting steps and fell at the feet of the two servants
his father had sent to him. They lifted him to his feet as if he
were a light and empty sack, and the older one said, "Everyone
is waiting for you, Francesco, everyone, especially your father
Pietro, and Donna Pica, your mother. They love you and are
bursting with happiness that you are at last freed from prison
and will again bring light to the family home."

"And where is home?" Francis asked. "No one sought me out,
no one tried to free me. I have no home; I have a house. And I
will return to my father's house."

The men gave each other knowing looks. This was not like
Francesco. Something bad, this terrible place, had changed him.

"It will be okay, Francesco. You just need to rest. You need time," the younger man said. "You've had a terrible experience. Did they torture you?"

"No. But the chains did, and the dark. I was in the dark much of the time. And my fellow prisoners made it worse with their curses, their moaning, their crying out in the night. I tried to cheer them. I sang for them. I encouraged them to keep hoping. But no one from Assisi came for us."

They were walking now, slowly, stumbling toward two horses tied nearby. It seemed too far to Francis, an impossible journey. But with the help of the steadying arms of his escorts, he made it to the horse he recognized as one of his favorite mounts before he'd gone to war. And the young mare, a white palfrey, recognized the young rider and began neighing and shaking her head.

He placed a shaking hand on the horse's neck, and the older man hoisted him onto the horse, then he mounted, as well, asking Francis to hold onto his waist. The younger man mounted the other horse and led the way, the three of them trotting slowly toward the town of Collestrada near Ponte San Giovanni on the same road that Francis walked with fellow Assisian soldiers the day, a year earlier, when they were taken prisoner by Perugian soldiers. He who had fancied himself a knight was forced to walk horseless and in defeat to what he thought would be death. And it was in a way much like death, that dark imprisonment.

And now he had emerged from that tomb and was going to a place that seemed foreign and threatening. He would have to act like his old self, and he knew he would not be able to do it. He only wanted to close his eyes and sleep.

And that is how he finally arrived again in Assisi, his mother and father laughing and weeping at the same time. And he could

not respond, except to ask to be taken to his bed. He asked
that the shutters be closed. He would, he said, be better in the
morning.

But he wasn't better. He felt worse. It must have been the seven-
teen miles on horseback, he thought. He only wanted to sleep,
and so he did. Sleep and have nightmares and fever. He could
taste his fear each morning, despite his mother's loving care and
his father's unusual patience as he waited for his former son to
emerge from his room alive and well, full of his old enthusiasm
and cheerfulness. He checked on Francis often, and Lady Pica
brought him food, cleaned and aired out the room. But Francis
could not interact with them, except to thank them and ask that
they let him rest. And the days dragged on, week after week,
month after month, until at last he woke to a morning without
fear, without, in fact, any feeling at all.

He sensed something had finally changed, and he wanted to
get up, to leave this cave of a room. He walked to the window
as if he were just learning to walk. He gently pushed open the
shutters and looked hopefully over the sunlit tiles of the city.
But he felt nothing. There was no joy, no sense of wonder and
awe as before when he'd wake full of anticipation of a new day,
eager for adventure. Now he could only dully scan the vista and
mechanically walk downstairs to where his parents waited hopefully, their forced smiles trying to rouse Francis from his torpor.

He kissed them without emotion and asked if might ride one
of his father's palfreys through the countryside. It was as if he
were asking his hosts if he could borrow one of their horses.

His father enthusiastically embraced his son. "*Si, si, Francesco*!
Take your pick. They are all yours. Ride, Francesco, ride!"

And so he did, day after day after day. He grew stronger. But
there was no joy. Perhaps if he got back on a warhorse again.

Maybe then he would feel once more the rush of adventure. And so it happened.

He heard, one day, that the great papal general, Walter of Brienne, was mounting a force in Apulia, and had sent out a call for troops to fight in the papal army. And to the delight of his father, Francis finally responded to something with enthusiasm. He began to sleep better, his nightmares replaced from time to time by dreams of glory like the one in which shields adorned with his own crest hung on a castle's walls, and he heard a voice saying that the shields were indeed for Francis and his followers. He determined to leave for Apulia as soon as his father—Pietro had become "his father" again—could supply the warhorse and armor. He would yet be a knight.

The early Franciscan chroniclers tell us what happened next, how Francis got to the town of Spoleto, only a day's journey from Assisi, and he had another dream, and in the dream he heard a voice:

> "Francis, What is better, to serve the master or the servant?"
> "Why, Sir, the master, of course."
> "Then why are you serving the servant? Return to Assisi, and it will be shown you what you are to do."

And so returning again in defeat to Assisi, looking to others like a coward who has returned home before even reaching the scene of battle, he began to wander about the countryside, walking at times, riding at others. He would ride and ride and ride. Ride to calm his nervous anxiety, ride to escape from the claustrophobic feel of life within the prison-like walls of Assisi, ride looking for someone on the road, some presence that would not fail him and leave him imprisoned. Maybe the voice in the dream would speak to him again. Maybe it wasn't just a real dream, but a delusion.

And then it happened. One day, on one of his interminable rides, he came upon a leper in the road and reined his horse to the side to avoid passing too close to the leper. But as he was about to ride past, he suddenly was moved to rein in his horse and dismount and, overcoming his terror and revulsion, to walk toward the leper. And when Francis was about to stretch out his hand to offer a coin, the leper offered his own hand expecting something. And Francis gave him both money and a kiss, and in that encounter Francis felt something momentous had happened. His heart had somehow changed, and he was filled with joy. And he knew where the joy came from because shortly afterward he went to the houses where the lepers lived, and he began to live among them, "working mercy with them," as he himself put it in his *Testament*. He had finally met Christ. He knew his face. He was a presence that was absence, an absence that was presence. But he had seen him among the lepers, though he had not yet heard his voice, unless the voice in the dream at Spoleto was the voice of Christ.

It turned out that it was indeed Christ's voice because he heard it again sometime later when he was praying in the dilapidated chapel of San Damiano outside the gates of Assisi and a short distance farther down the hillside of Mount Subasio. He had prayed there before, but all was silence. This time, however, as he prayed before the neglected Byzantine crucifix that hung above the altar, his eyes fixed upon the crucified image of the broken Christ he had already met in the lepers, suddenly the image of Christ began to speak and it was indeed the voice he'd heard in the dream at Spoleto, this time with a new message: "Francis, go and repair my house, which as you see, is falling into ruins."

Then all was silence again, except for the scratching voices of the cicadas outside, which Francis did not hear at first, so absorbed was he in the voice of Christ echoing over and over the halls of his memory. He had been told, by Christ himself, what it was he was to do, just as Christ had promised in Spoleto. He'd been given a task. It was not what he thought he'd hear if ever God spoke to him. It was not how he imagined it would be. But it was enough. He had touched God in the leper, and now he had heard God's voice speak from the dirt-encrusted cross of San Damiano.

He rose quickly and bowed deeply to the crucified image of Christ and ran from the small church. He sped up the hill and through the gates to his father's shop where he took a bolt of cloth and, jumping onto his horse, raced to the neighboring town of Foligno. There he sold the cloth and the horse and walked briskly back to Assisi, to the small church of San Damiano, intending to give the money to the poor priest who resided there and ask him to use the money to repair the church, as Christ himself had commanded to be done.

But the priest would have none of it. He feared Francis's father, the rich cloth merchant, Pietro Bernardone; and he had heard of this capricious son of Bernardone who had lost his mind and now haunted poor churches looking for God. He refused Francis's offer of money, which Francis then threw onto the windowsill of the church and hurried up the hill to Assisi to beg stones to repair the church himself. While he worked, the poor priest let him stay with him, at least while he pursued his mad effort to repair the church with whatever stones he could find or beg.

Absence was beginning to be replaced by presence, silence with voices. Or were the voices only in his head? Whatever. They moved him to act, to do positive things with his life, a pattern Francis would follow from then on. Once he knew God's will, whether from some mystical voice or from listening to the scriptures, he would immediately try to live it out. He was filled with what theologians called, "devotion," an alacrity in doing God's will.

And that is how Francis began to change. He knew now that Christ is to be found in unexpected places and people. He had experienced the abstract God in the person of Jesus Christ who was the incarnation of the God he thought had abandoned him. And he had experienced this Jesus in the most excluded and feared people of his time, the lepers who, instead of bad things, brought him the greatest good, Jesus Christ. And now he had heard the voice of this Christ. It came from his crucified image in an abandoned church. It was a voice that gave him his life's task: "Go and repair my house, which, as you see, is falling into ruins."

Repairing the actual structure, the walls and roof, of the small chapel of San Damiano, was both a physical task and a metaphor for repairing the universal Church itself, as was evident when he went to Rome to have his Rule of Life approved by Pope Innocent III.

The night before he gave his approval, Pope Innocent had a dream in which he saw the Roman church of St. John Lateran, the mother church of all churches, threatening to fall down, but a small beggar was keeping it from falling by shoring it up with his shoulder.

The practical conclusion of the first teaching of St. Francis is that if we listen and pray, God will show us what we are to do with our lives. In Francis's life it had to do with intimacy with God in God's Son, Jesus Christ, whom he found first in the lepers, and then in repairing the dwelling place of God; first in God's churches and then in repairing the believing community, the Mystical Body of Christ, which is the Church. The latter rebuilding had to do with repairing human relationships by, in Francis's words, "working mercy" with them. God indwells churches as he indwelled the Ark of the Covenant. God indwells people just as he had first become human in Jesus Christ. And God indwells the gathering of believers, which we call the Church, which is the Mystical Body of Christ, the fullness of the Incarnation of God.

The Wisdom of St. Francis

We thank you
that through your Son you created us,
and that through the holy love you had for us
you brought about his birth
as true God and true man
by the glorious, ever virgin, most blessed, holy Mary ...
—Rule of 1221, Chapter XXIII

We are mothers of our Lord Jesus Christ when we carry him in our hearts and in our bodies, lovingly, and with a pure and sincere conscience, and give birth to him through the working of his grace in us which should shine forth as an example to others.
—Letter to All the Faithful, Second Version

We are his spouses when our faithful souls are wed to
Jesus Christ by the Holy Spirit. We are his brothers
and sisters when we do the will of his Father who is in
heaven.

—Letter to All the Faithful, Second Version

Behold the Word of the Father, so worthy, so holy
and glorious, whose coming the Most High Father
announced from heaven in the womb of the holy and
glorious Virgin Mary through his holy angel Gabriel!
From the Virgin Mary's womb he received our human
flesh and frailty. 'Although he was rich' (2 Corinthians
8:9) and was placed above all things, he nevertheless
decided with the Most Blessed Virgin Mary his mother,
to choose poverty in this world.

—Letter to All the Faithful, Second Version

Francis used to observe with inexpressible eagerness,
and above all other solemnities the Birth of the Child
Jesus, calling it the feast of feasts on which God, having
become a little baby, hung upon human breasts. He
would avidly kiss pictures of those infant limbs, and his
compassion for the child overflowed his heart, making
him stammer sweet words, even like a child. The name
Baby Jesus was for him honeycomb-sweet in the mouth.

—Thomas of Celano, *Second Life of St. Francis*, 199

If I ever have the opportunity to talk with the emperor,
I'll beg him, for the love of God and me, to enact a
special law: No one is to capture or kill our sisters the
larks or do them any harm. Furthermore, all mayors
and lords of castles and towns are to be required each

year on Christmas Day to order their subjects to scatter wheat and other grain on the roads outside the walls so that our sisters the larks and other birds might have something to eat on so festive a day. And on Christmas Eve, out of reverence for the Son of God, whom on that night the Virgin Mary placed in a manger between the ox and the ass, anyone having an ox or an ass is to feed it a generous portion of choice fodder. And on Christmas Day the rich are to give the poor the finest food in abundance.

—*Mirror of Perfection*, 14

A Christmas Psalm of St. Francis

Sing for joy to God our strength (Ps 81:1),
  acclaim the Lord God living and true with shouts of
  joy (cf. Ps 47:1).

For Yahweh, the Most High, is glorious,
  the great king over all the earth (Ps 37:2).

Because the Most Holy Father of Heaven, our king from
the first (cf. Ps 74:12),
  sent his beloved Son from on high, and he was born of
  the blessed, holy Virgin Mary.

"He will cry to me, 'You are my Father'...
  So I shall make him my first-born, the highest of
  earthly kings" (Ps. 89:26-27).

On that day the Lord bestowed his mercy and that night
his song (cf. Ps 42:8).

This is the day, which Yahweh has made,
    a day for us to rejoice and be glad (Ps 118:24).

For the Most Holy Beloved Child was given to us and
was born for us (cf. Is 9:5)
    on the way and was laid for us in a manger, because
    there was no room at the inn (cf. Lk 2:7).

—Office of the Passion

Let humanity kneel in fear, let the whole universe
tremble, and let heaven rejoice when Christ the Son of
the Living God is on the altar in the hands of the priest!

O wonderful ascent, O stupendous descent! O sublime
humility! O humble sublimity that the Lord of the
Universe, God and Son of God, should so humbly hide
himself for our salvation in what seems to be only a
small piece of bread! Look, then, upon the humility of
God! And pour out your hearts before him. Humble
yourselves that he might exalt you. Hold back nothing
of yourselves for yourselves, that he may receive your all
who gave his all to you.

—Letter to the Whole Order

SECOND TEACHING

The Paradox of Evangelical Poverty

THE SECOND TEACHING OF ST. FRANCIS IS that we find God when we become poor enough for God to find us. For God is a humble God, as powerless as one hanging on a cross, hands and feet bound, unable to strike out, or strike back. And in that lowly poverty of the seemingly powerless God is the greatest power of all, the mystery of the Divine powerless power to transform all things, including the wayward human heart.

Usually, when people think of St. Francis, they think of the saint of animals, the saint of the birdbath; or they think of a poor beggar who had renounced wealth and power to live a life of Gospel poverty. Both images are true, but here it is the image of the poverty of St. Francis that I turn to the imagination to help illumine.

He felt so young, so inexperienced in the ways of God with human beings. He needed the guidance of God's word. He needed to hear the Holy Gospel read out in the mass. He hungered for the word of God, just as he hungered for the Holy Eucharist. They kept him alive; they nourished his soul.

And so he wandered the countryside, he visited abandoned churches, he attended Holy Mass whenever he could, and he repaired San Damiano and two other churches, including the small chapel of St. Mary of the Angels on the plain below Assisi. And it happened one day in this same church of St. Mary of the Angels, on the feast of St. Matthias the Apostle, that Francis was at mass when the words of the Gospel for that feast day suddenly struck like a flaming sword penetrating to the depths of his being. He lost all consciousness of anything else but the sweet pain of the words' resonance in his heart. In the story inside the words Christ was sending forth his disciples to preach, and he was telling them how they were to go along the roads of their preaching missions. They were not to keep gold or silver in their belts, nor were they to have a wallet for their journey. They were not to have two tunics, nor shoes, nor staff.

Were he not already standing, Francis would have risen to his feet and proclaimed aloud, "This is what I want, this is what I desire with all my heart!"

And that was the beginning of the form of life that Francis embraced, a poor life, an Apostolic life of being sent by Christ to go forth on the roads of the world to preach the Gospel while carrying as little baggage as possible. It was a way of life that was further defined for Francis when his first companion, the rich and respected citizen of Assisi, Bernard of Quintavalle, came to Francis and asked to join him in living a life consecrated to God.

In response to Bernard's question of what he had to do to join Francis, Francis did what he continued to do for the rest of his life: He turned to the book of the Gospels to hear what Christ had to say. And this is what Francis and Bernard found in the Gospel when they went to the Assisi church of St. Nicholas and prayed that God would enlighten them. With the guidance of the priest they opened the book three times, and on the first opening, the text that Christ gave them was, "If you wish to be perfect, go and sell all you own, and give to the poor." They closed the book joyfully and opened it a second time to these words: "Take nothing for your journey." With their hearts burning with love, they opened the book a final time and heard Christ speak to them the words inside the other two admonitions he had given them: "If you would follow me, deny yourself and take up your cross and follow me." With great joy Francis turned to Bernard and said, "This, then, is our life and rule." And Bernard and Francis went to the fountain in the Piazza del Comune of Assisi and gave away all of Bernard's belongings. And that was the beginning of what we call today "Franciscan Poverty."

Francis and Bernard did what all Franciscans after them have tried to do, Franciscan men and women of all three Orders that St. Francis founded: the Friars, the Poor Clares, and the Secular Franciscans who live out the Franciscan Rule and Life given to Francis and Bernard in the church of St. Nicholas in Assisi. It is a way of life based on what Jesus himself did.

It is a way of life in imitation of Jesus, the Humble God, who, in Paul's words to the Philippians, though he was in the form of God did not cling to divinity but emptied himself becoming obedient to God and humans, obedient even to death on a cross (cf. Philippians 2:6-8.) Franciscans are about self-emptying in imitation of the self-emptying, the *kenosis*, of Jesus Christ.

For Francis and Bernard this self-emptying began with divesting themselves of wealth, for they were both wealthy men. They had everything that is supposed to make one happy, but they were not happy. They were too full of self and possessiveness to receive the riches of Christ. They had to make themselves empty enough for the humble God to enter and fill their emptiness.

And everyone seeking to be a Franciscan today, in one way or another asks herself or himself two questions: "What is it I am holding onto too tightly for the Humble God to find a space within me?" And secondly, "What did St. Francis do and why did he do it?"

I believe the answer to these two questions can be traced back to the beginning of his conversion when his father reacted to Francis's going through the streets of Assisi begging stones to repair the small church of San Damiano. When Francis would not stop what his father considered shameful and aberrant behavior, Pietro dragged him home and imprisoned him, as had the Perugians.

Few punishments could have more traumatic. He was again in terror. He could not escape from the small claustrophobic space within his own home. His mother, Lady Pica, brought him food and water; and when Pietro left for another cloth-buying trip, she unchained and released Francis. He fled immediately to San Damiano to continue his work on the church.

For Pietro that was the final straw, and when he returned, he summoned Francis before the civil authorities so that they could judge concerning Pietro's grievances against his wayward son. But Francis refused to appear, saying he was now under the jurisdiction of the Church and accordingly would appear only before the bishop. And that is what happened.

And so it was before the bishop's court that Pietro demanded of Francis that he return the money and possessions that belonged rightfully to his father. Then, in a scene celebrated in art and literature, Francis returned not only his father's money, but, stripping himself of his clothes, he lay them at the feet of his cloth merchant father. The bishop rushed forward and covered Francis's nakedness, and Francis said to his father for all to hear, "Until now I have called you father here on earth, but now I can say without reservation, 'Our Father who art in heaven (Mt 6:9), since I have placed all my treasure and my hope in him."[2]

Francis had renounced his father, his patrimony, and embraced God as his all. It was that shocking and radical act that set the tone for Francis's following of the Poor Christ, who had emptied himself of his divine trappings in order to come among us and love us. The difference between Christ's self-emptying and Francis's was that Christ was sent by the Father and was one with the Father. Francis rejected his own father and chose to embrace Christ's Father as his father.

That was the pivotal moment when Francis left the world, the world being the values of his father and of the city that gave him birth. And he left by descending to the lepers and to all the rejected, marginal people who live outside and below the walls of wealth, privilege and self-importance. He was doing what Christ did, going down in order to rise again, even from death itself.

That is the heart of Franciscan poverty, that self-emptying, that *kenosis* akin to Christ's own self-emptying in the Incarnation.

How Francis learned of Christ's *kenosis* was his going among the lepers. His most personal and intense summary of this extraordinary and revelatory time in his life appears in the first section of his *Testament*.

He says:

> For I, being in sin, thought it bitter to look at lepers.
> And the Lord himself led me among them, and I worked

mercy with them. And when I left their company, I realized that what had seemed bitter to me, had been turned into sweetness of soul and body.[3]

The *Testament* was written in his final days—he died on October 3, 1226. It is a letter of reminiscences, such as the one above, a series of exhortations and commands for his brothers, and a plea for poverty, even as the Order changed from no buildings or churches of their own to churches and buildings that, to Francis, were not in accord with the poverty they had promised in the Rule. He emphasizes that even in poor dwellings and poor churches they are always to be guests there as the pilgrims and strangers they are.

The exhortations, such as the ones here, reveal what his preoccupations had been since his return from Egypt and the Fifth Crusade in 1219 and his calling of an emergency chapter of the order in 1220, six years before his *Testament,* a title that could also mean "covenant," namely the brothers' covenant with God when they made their vows.

He is preoccupied with buildings because while he was away in the Holy Land, certain brothers began leading the order in a direction that Francis saw as a betrayal of the Gospel poverty and simplicity of the original vision God had given to him. Francis heard of this development when he was still in Egypt. One of the brothers had made his way there to alert Francis to what was going on during his absence, and Francis returned with the brother-messenger to Italy where they landed in Venice. They then made their way to Bologna where Francis avoided the new house of studies the brothers had built there.

The following year in the Chapter of the Brothers in Assisi Francis spoke forcefully against the friars who were abandoning the original charism of the order and forthwith resigned as minister and servant of all the friars. Cardinal Hugolino, the protector of the order and who later became Pope Gregory IX, was present; and some of the learned brothers asked the cardinal to try to persuade Francis to follow their advice regarding the future direction of the order, which would make their Rule more closely aligned to the great Rules and practices already being lived in the Church.

Francis listened, then took Cardinal Hugolino by the hand and led him before the assembled brothers. Then Francis spoke in words that are at the heart of all the teachings of St. Francis:

> "My brothers, my brothers, God called me to walk in the way of humility and showed me the way of simplicity. I do not want to hear any mention of the rule of St. Augustine, of St. Bernard, or of St. Benedict. The Lord has told me that he wanted to make a new fool of me in the world, and God does not want to lead us by any other knowledge than that. God will use your personal knowledge and your wisdom to confound you; he has policemen to punish you, and I put my trust in him. Then in your shame you will return to your first state, whether you like it or not!" The cardinal, dumbfounded, kept silence, and all the brothers were gripped by fear.[4]

Around these words of St. Francis controversies within the order he founded began to swirl, not only around the interpretation of the Franciscan Rule, especially with regard to poverty, but also around St. Francis himself. Who was he? What is an accurate and true story of his life? These controversies grew so intense during the final years of the thirteenth century that St.

Bonaventure, who was at that time the successor to St. Francis as leader of the order, and the chapter of the order itself, had to draft a new set of constitutions for interpreting and living the Franciscan Rule. St. Bonaventure himself was commissioned by the chapter to write a definitive life of St. Francis that would supplant all the previous *Lives*, which he faithfully fulfilled, using the extant sources, especially the two Lives by Brother Thomas of Celano and the testimonies of the early brothers that in time came to bear the names of Leo, Angelo, and Rufino, though other brothers gave testimony as well.

All this flurry of activity was undertaken to bring some kind of unity to the Franciscan Order and a reliable account of the life and writings of its founder, St. Francis. But, as with Christianity itself, different readings of the life, writings, and message of its founder persist into our own time.

Sadly for Franciscans, these disparate readings made for centuries of controversy over the meaning and practice of the poverty that the brothers vow to keep. I say "sadly," because poverty itself is not the center of who Franciscans are. Jesus Christ is the center; and it is in holding on to him and his Gospel as it was heard and lived by St. Francis as our guide and ideal that we grow in holiness and love. No matter whose interpretation is in vogue or who is telling the story of St. Francis, what matters is whether or not our living out of St. Francis's teachings and example bring us closer to Christ and to the love of God. There is faith, hope, and love, St. Paul counsels, and the greatest of these is love, the love we call charity.

And as for poverty, it seems that our focus should not be on things, whether they be material or spiritual, and whether or not we have them, but on whether or not we appropriate them to ourselves when they are, in fact, God's gifts. It is *appropriatio*, the term St. Francis uses, "appropriation," that is the essence of whether or not one has the spirit of Evangelical Poverty. Appropriation is not measurable, the way property or money is measurable. It is a matter of the heart and mind and soul. Do I appropriate to myself what belongs to God? "My talent, my mind, my friary, my opinions, my car, my money, my, my my." And if I do possess these things, how tightly do I hold on? Will being separated from whatever I cling to bring me death or life?

Separation from the things of the world brought St. Francis life, but it also made him a new kind of fool. We say to ourselves, "Nobody takes things to the extremes that St. Francis did. It's crazy, foolish. His was indeed a special grace." And, of course, it was a unique grace. But, as Francis said to his brothers toward the end of his life, "I have done what was mine to do; may the Lord show you what is yours." And the Lord does, to those open to God's grace. Our individual response is unique, but if we also belong to a religious order, like the Franciscans, it is also a communal response, and we strive to find a commonality of response we can all agree on. That struggle is where charity and love enter and, hopefully, prevail over the differences.

For those who are not members of the orders St. Francis founded, Franciscans try to be examples of simplified, poor lives of service to others, rich and poor alike. And Franciscans try to remember the poor, materially and spiritually, and bring them Christ and his Gospel. And they endeavor to do this as brothers and/or sisters who have embraced the life and Rule of Life that Francis of Assisi gave us as our map for living a full God-centered life.

The Wisdom of St. Francis

God is well pleased with poverty, and above all with *voluntary* poverty. For my part I possess royal dignity and special nobility in that I follow the Lord, who was rich but became poor for "our sakes" (cf. 2 Corinthians 8:9).

I have never been a thief of alms, seeking or using more than I needed. I have always accepted less than was necessary, lest other poor people be cheated of their share.

—*Mirror of Perfection, 12*

As far as the brothers distance themselves from poverty, that far will the world distance itself from the brothers, and they will search and not find (cf. Lk 11:10). But if they remain in the embrace of my Lady Poverty, the world will nourish them, for then they are given the world for its salvation.

—Thomas of Celano, *Second Life of St. Francis, 70*

In the medieval allegory, *Sacrum Commercium (Holy Exchange)*, St. Francis addresses Lady Poverty, Christ's Bride:

You, most faithful spouse, sweetest lover, were never for one moment separated from your Lord. In fact, you clung all the more fiercely to him, the more others despised him. Of course, had you not been with him, he would not have been so despised by all.

You were with him amid the shouts and insults of the Pharisees, the reproaches of the chief priests; you were with him buffeted and spit upon and scourged.

He deserved the veneration of all; he received mockery instead, and you alone comforted him. You did not abandon him, "even to accepting death, death on a cross" (Philippians 2:8). And on the cross, when his body hung there naked, his arms outstretched, his hands and feet nailed to the wood, you suffered with him, and nothing appeared more glorious in him than you.

Then when he went to heaven, he left with you the seal of the kingdom of heaven so that you could seal the elect. Whoever, then, would sigh for the eternal kingdom must come to you, must ask you for it, and must enter it through you, for no one can enter the kingdom without the imprint of your seal.

—*Sacrum Commercium, 2–21*

The Bishop of Assisi once said to St. Francis, "I think your life is too hard, too rough. You don't possess anything in this world."

And St. Francis replied, "My Lord, if we had possessions, we would need weapons to defend them."

—*The Anonymous of Perugia, Chapter III, 17*

You eat from the Tree of the Knowledge of Good when you appropriate to yourself your own will, thus crediting yourself with the good which the Lord says and does in you.

—*Admonition, 2*

Third Teaching

Live the Gospel

"As we forgive those who trespass against us," and what
we do not fully forgive, O Lord, make us fully forgive,
so that for your sake, we may truly love our enemies and
devoutly intercede for them with you, thereby rendering
no evil for evil, but striving in you to do good to all...
—St. Francis, Paraphrase of the Our Father

In his writings and in the early biographies of St. Francis, he
emerges as a person formed and informed by the Gospel of Jesus
Christ. What does that mean? How do we even begin to live the
Gospel, as he did, in our own time? We delight in Francis's playfulness and in his joyful response to beauty and goodness, but
like us, he also had to struggle with the harder questions posed
by the Gospels. It is the implications of these more difficult questions that I would like to explore in this chapter on living the
Gospel today.

One cold January night when the world seemed to lie in darkness,
I sat down from a long day and turned to C-Span2, BookTV.
One of the books that piqued my interest was James H. Cone's,

The Cross and the Lynching Tree. I'd not heard of it before, and as the book was being discussed, something awakened in me, and I saw how vacuous was the Christmas I had participated in a few weeks before. Even though I was centered on the Christ Child and the Franciscan emphasis on the Incarnation, it was a sentimental Baby Jesus who filled my prayer and my imagination—not the baby who grew and matured and gave us the Sermon on the Mount which he then lived out and because of which he was put to death on the hanging tree of the cross. I was looking at the Baby Jesus of countless crèches and not at the babies who were slain by King Herod because of the Baby Jesus.

The Christmas I'd celebrated was in the midst of a frenzied commercialism equaled only by the despair of so many who had lost homes and jobs and dignity in support of an imperfect and money-corrupted government that insists on supporting an often selfish and corrupt corporate empire that controls the world. The implications of the connections between Jesus in the crib and Jesus on the cross, like someone hanged from a tree, are overshadowed and seem, at times, almost eradicated by the world that our greed, self-interest, and neglect of the poor and the disenfranchised have created.

St. Francis saw the connection between the crib and the cross. Brother Thomas of Celano, in his first life of St. Francis, said of the live Christmas crib which Francis began near the town of Greccio, in the very center of Italy:

> His greatest care, his most vivid desire, his supreme resolution was to observe the holy Gospel always and in everything and with all vigilance and care, with all of his mind's desire and his heart's fervor, he wanted to follow the teachings and imitate the examples of our Lord Jesus

Christ to perfection. He continuously recalled and medi-
tated over His words and with very keen contemplation,
he kept His works before his eyes.

*The humility of the Incarnation and the charity of
the Passion* were foremost in his mind, so that he rarely
wanted to think of anything else. (my italics)[5]

And so we ask ourselves, what is to be done, what can we do to
bring the Christ of the Gospel back into Christmas in a way that
is more than a bumper sticker slogan that ends up being mainly
a political football? How can we bring the Christ of the Gospel
back into our daily lives so that we actually live out the teachings
of the Gospel where we first learned the story of Christ?

In the quote above Brother Thomas says of St. Francis, "His
greatest care, his most vivid desire, his supreme resolution was
to observe the holy Gospel...." And this very Gospel emphasizes over and over again the imperative of reaching out to those
who, like the man in Jesus's parable of the Good Samaritan, have
fallen among thieves, which in turn calls to mind the rapacious-
ness of those forces and structures that control our economy
and of the many who are left by the wayside. How, then, can we
today reach out to those fallen and to the thieves, as well?

St. John the Evangelist tells us that the truth will set us free.
But what does that mean? St. Francis found the truth that leads
to freedom in the truths of the Gospel, and the freedom he found
was the freedom to love. God's truth imparts to us the freedom
not only to grasp the truth that is being imparted but also the
freedom from what previously had been preventing us from
acting on that truth. The Gospel itself will show us not only how
we are to discern the truth, but how the truth leads to the action
we call love.

For, from the beginning of his conversion, Francis learned and teaches us that truth-hearing and truth-telling are not enough. Words are never enough. As St. John says further in his First Letter: "How does God's love abide in anyone who has the world's goods and sees a brother or sister in need and yet refuses help? Little children, let us love, not in word or speech, but in truth and action. And by this we will know that we are from the truth and will reassure our hearts before him" (1 John 3:17–19).

There is a charming story in Brother Thomas of Celano's first Life of St. Francis that illustrates St. Francis's care for the poor.

> It happened once that the mother of two of the brothers came to St. Francis and his companions seeking alms. Now St. Francis used to call the mother of any of the brothers his mother and the mother of all the brothers. But when this poor woman came seeking alms, Francis was sad because they had nothing in the house but the New Testament which they used for prayer. So he said to his vicar, Brother Peter: "Give our mother the New Testament. And let her sell it to take care of her needs. I'm sure it is more pleasing to God that we give away the New Testament we use for prayer than hold on to it. After all, it is this very book that teaches us to help the poor."[6]

St. Francis would not let this poor mother fall by the wayside. He knew from the Gospels themselves that whatever falls by the wayside and dies because of our negligence and indifference and silence is somehow our responsibility if we knew about it and could have done something to prevent it—even if that is only the deed of our prayers of intercession and/or of our refusal to concur with those policies which disenfranchise and make invisible the poor among us. But St. Francis did more than pray or not keep silent; he helped the poor woman herself, providing her with something she could sell to provide for her needs. From his own inner conversion he knew with certainty that this was what he should do to help the poor mother of two of his brothers. He knew that this was Gospel love.

Without the kind of internal conversion of heart that Francis came to in his own life, we can easily find our certainties elsewhere, even from those who have elevated their own opinions and prejudices to the level of truth. And without our own inner certainties we can easily start listening to these false truths of others, often listening to the loudest, most convincing speaker rather than listening to God in the silence in which God speaks to the depths of the soul. And then we begin to imitate others' words and actions, as if they are our own hard-won truths and ways of living that we have come to after pondering prayerfully and carefully what is said and acted upon by others.

So, if we are to learn from St. Francis today and live the words of Christ in the Gospel, we need first of all to ask what part we ourselves may be playing in disseminating lies without considering more carefully whether or not they are the truth they pretend to be, or being silent when we know lies are being proclaimed as the truth. And then, seeking God's mercy and forgiveness, like St. Francis, we try to begin again, listening to the words of the Gospel to find the truth, praying over them, and living them out in our daily lives, all the while asking God to help us to be people of the truth who try always to speak the truth.

We all sin with our tongues to one degree or another, but to act as if it is okay to say something is true, even if we're not sure it is true, is a dangerous practice. It can lead to thinking and acting as if careless, unkind, and untrue statements about others that reinforce our own prejudices or fears somehow absolve us from the discipline of discerning truth from falsehood and give us free reign to say anything we want about someone, whether or not we know that it is true. As long as we "feel" it's true, or it "could" be true, or we want it to be true, we can think it is okay to speak of it as true. Most social sin has its roots in some lie that has been declared true by unscrupulous people whose morality is that whatever they say is moral is thereby moral, usually backed up by someone considered an expert, but who could actually be someone who has become his or her own truth.

This kind of refusal to examine the truth or falsehood of what is being said is a serious obstacle to true dialogue and understanding among people because it inhibits real listening to the other. And without dialogue and sincere efforts to bring peace and reconciliation among people, there is no charity, no real community of peoples, and everything turns hostile and lines are drawn in the sand, and weapons are taken up, and wars begin that could have been avoided. And today, with the possibility of nuclear annihilation, war is not the first option, or any reasonable option at all.

To some what I have just written may sound quite negative and not "Franciscan"; and I realize that the danger of concentrating on the negative is that it may bring us to become what we most dislike and criticize. But I am also aware of and try to concentrate more on the truth that there is always a counter valence to evil and darkness; and that positive vision, that lens, is what the Franciscan vision emphasizes: light and lightheartedness that keep trying to see and become light and beauty and goodness that the darkness cannot overcome. It is the light that ultimately is Christ and the Good News that he is the Son of God and has risen from the dead, as we, too, will rise. It is the belief that this truth will transform us and keep us positive and lightsome, even in the face of darkness that at times we need to name in order to grow into the light again.

For example, as I sit here writing, the black ink blotting the yellow legal pad, I look up and out my small hermitage window to a blast of red bougainvillea petals. Out of the corner of my vision through the glass door of the room I also can see the week's trash overflowing a black, plastic tub. I'm aware the black tub is there, but I stare at the red petals, though the sun is illumining both. I see and acknowledge and will attend to the black tub's trash. I see and I stare at the bougainvillea. There is a balance in that way of seeing that I hope the rest of this book reflects and illumines.

This preference for light and beauty is one of the reasons St. Francis is attractive to us and why he was so successfully a peacemaker in his own time. It is why today his town of Assisi has been the site of peace conferences and prayer meetings to promote peace. St. Francis is seen as the gentle saint who shows us that the way to peace and justice is the way Christ has shown us in the Gospels, namely, the way of the love of God, which is THE way; and its companion is the way of love of our neighbor as ourselves.

This basic Gospel truth is the message of the Gospel St. Francis finally was able to hear in the Gospel he lived and preached. He learned that if we put those two commandments in precisely that order, we easily see how and when we sin in departing from the truth and in hurting our neighbor. All truth is from God, and

God's truth is that we are to love God, and loving God will show us how to love our neighbor. Living the Gospel must start with embracing this basic Gospel truth. Only then will we, too, begin to hear the voice of God.

There will, of course, always be false prophets and deceivers, "wolves in sheep's clothing," Jesus called them. But this does not mean that we are to go about criticizing and correcting; that only separates further. It is only necessary to be true to oneself; and if it is called for, to speak our own understanding of what the truth is without denigrating others. Peace is achieved more effectively by trying to bring out the best, not pointing out the worst, in others. And we bring out the best in others by being ourselves peaceful. Our own peaceful presence will do more than trying to persuade others that we are right and they are wrong. Peacefulness is its own persuasion.

That is the best option, it seems to me, for those committed to living the Gospel. The Franciscan response to sin and division is to forgive myself and my neighbor, thereby becoming peaceful in my own center, and then to reach out to others and "work mercy" with them, even with those whom I find it difficult to love, who repel me in any way. We work together toward the good, or we perish as individuals, as societies and as civilizations.

Saint Francis began a new evangelization in his own time, not by trying to be social reformer. He simply loved Christ and lived the Gospel, and he and his brothers became thereby catalysts for social change. They became "Holy Fools" who turned the world upside down by simply living the truth of the Gospel of Christ.

Like Francis and his brothers, we all *can* learn to love again, even in the midst of division and war. And the map Francis gave us for learning to love is the Gospel and his own life of following in the footsteps of Christ. This map has been summed up beautifully in his Peace Prayer, a prayer he did not write but certainly is the way he prayed and lived and taught by example. It is a prayer that outlines everything that made Francis the peacemaker that he was and the model for peace that he is for us today. It is a prayer that shows us how to find the truth again, if we've lost it, or to continue living in the truth we've already found and are trying to live.

> Lord, make me an instrument of your peace:
>> where there is hatred, let me sow love;
>> where there is injury, pardon;
>> where there doubt, faith;
>> where there is despair, hope;
>> where there is darkness, light;
>> and where there is sadness, joy.
> O Divine Master, grant that I may not so much seek
>> to be consoled, as to console,
>> to be understood, as to understand,
>> to be loved, as to love.
>> For it is in giving that we receive,
>> it is in pardoning that we are pardoned,
>> and it is in dying that we are born to eternal life.

Building upon this prayer, on January 24, 2018, Pope Francis issued a statement and a new prayer he wrote for World Communications Day celebrated on May 13, 2018. The statement and the prayer are helpful antidotes to the phenomenon that Pope Francis defines as untruth and the spreading of disinformation. It has to do with false information based on non-existent or distorted data meant to deceive and manipulate the reader. Spreading fake news can serve to advance specific goals, influence political decisions, and serve economic interests. The effectiveness of fake news is primarily due to its ability to *mimic* real news, to seem plausible. Secondly, this false but believable news is "captious," inasmuch as it grasps people's attention by appealing to stereotypes and common social prejudices, and exploiting instantaneous emotions like anxiety, contempt, anger and frustration. The ability to spread such fake news often relies on a manipulative use of the social networks and the way they function. Untrue stories can spread so quickly that even authoritative denials fail to contain the damage.

...The tragedy of disinformation is that it discredits others, presenting them as enemies, to the point of demonizing them and fomenting conflict. Fake news is a sign of intolerant and hypersensitive attitudes, and leads only to the spread of arrogance and hatred. That is the end result of untruth.

According to Pope Francis, the antidote is not some new technique of discernment but people: "people who are not greedy but ready to listen, people who make the effort to engage in sincere dialogue so that the truth can emerge; people who are attracted by goodness and take responsibility for how they use language."

In pursuit of that end, Pope Francis gives all of us his new prayer that draws upon the Peace Prayer of St. Francis:

Lord, make us instruments of your peace.
Help us to recognize the evil latent in a communication
that does not build communion.
Help us to remove the venom from our judgments.
Help us to speak about others as our brothers and
sisters.
You are faithful and trustworthy; may our words be
seeds of goodness for the world:
    where there is shouting, let us practice listening;
    where there is confusion, let us inspire harmony;
    where there is ambiguity, let us bring clarity;
    where there is exclusion, let us offer solidarity;
    where there is sensationalism, let us use sobriety;
    where there is superficiality, let us raise real
      questions;
    where there is prejudice, let us awaken trust;
    where there is hostility, let us bring respect;
    where there is falsehood, let us bring truth.
Amen.[7]

—Pope Francis

THE WISDOM OF ST. FRANCIS

Let your discourse be brief, because the Lord's words were few when he was on earth. – Rule of 1223, Chapter IX

And after the Lord gave me some brothers, no one showed me what to do; but the Most High revealed to me that I was to live according to the Gospel. And I had it written down in brief, simple words, and the Lord Pope confirmed it for me.

And those who came to receive this life gave everything they had to the poor; and they were happy with
one tunic patched inside and out, and with a cord and
breeches.And we had no desire for anything else.

—*The Testament* of St. Francis

To all Christians: religious, clerics, and lay people, men
and women; to all who inhabit the whole world, Brother
Francis, your servant and subject, offers the homage of
reverence, true peace from heaven, and sincere love in
the Lord. Since I am everyone's servant, I am bound to
serve and minister to everyone the fragrant words of my
Lord.

—Letter to All the Faithful, Second Version.

At one time St Francis struggled within himself whether
he should live a life of contemplation or the life of a
preacher. He shared his struggle with the brothers close
to him saying,

In prayer we talk to God and listen to him, and we walk
with the angels. But in preaching, we have to descend
to the human and live among others as one of them,
thinking and seeing and hearing and speaking only on
the human level. But, in favor of preaching, there is one
argument which seems to count more than all the rest in
God's eyes and it is this: the only-begotten Son of God,
who is Infinite Wisdom, descended from the Father's
embrace to save souls. He renewed the world by his own
example, bringing the word of salvation among human
beings. The price of this salvation was his Precious
Blood, which washes us clean, and is a fortifying drink.

He kept nothing for himself, but generously gave his all for our salvation. We then are bound to act always according to the model which we see shining in him as on a high mountain. Therefore it seems more in accord with God's will that I leave the repose of contemplation and go out into the world to work.

—St. Bonaventure, *Major Life of Saint Francis,* 12:1

The Lord revealed to me that this is to be our greeting: "The Lord give you peace."

—*The Testament* of St. Francis

Every evening a herald should proclaim or use some other signal to announce to all the people that they are to render praise and thanks to the Lord God Almighty.

—Letter to the Rulers of the People

All-powerful, eternal, just, and merciful God, grant that we poor creatures might do, by your grace, what we know you want us to do, and to want always what is pleasing to you, so that interiorly cleansed and enlightened, and inflamed by the fire of the Holy Spirit, we might follow the footsteps of your Beloved Son, our Lord Jesus Christ, and by your grace alone come to you, O Most High, you who live and reign glorified in perfect Trinity and simple Unity, God Almighty, forever and ever. Amen.

—Letter to the Whole Order

I admonish you and encourage you in Christ to show all possible reverence for the written words of God wherever you may find them; and if you come upon God's words, and you see that they are not being cared for or are piled up sloppily or are scattered about, gather them up and care for them, for in honoring the words, you honor the Lord who spoke them.

—Letter to the Whole Order

FOURTH TEACHING

Go and Repair God's House

BERNARD OF THE QUINTAVALLE DI BERARDELLO FAMILY knew Francis of the Pietro Bernardone family from afar. They were both from the emerging merchant class; and as they were growing up, the more serious Bernard would watch Francis, the leader of the rowdy, boisterous youth of Assisi who would sing and dance through the streets after dark. Bernard, sensibly at home, would sit at his window and watch and listen, as during the day he would go about the serious business of fostering his family's honor and prestige among the citizens of Assisi. So much so, that by the time Francis began to change drastically from the seemingly carefree man-about-town to the town beggar and fool, Bernard was already a distinguished young man, known for his learning, a man who held degrees in both civil and canon law.

Bernard was appalled at the change in Francis, who was mocked and spit upon as he walked threadbare through the streets of Assisi, begging stones for the repair of the little church of San Damiano outside the walls. Francis had become a young man obsessed with begging and building and identifying with the poor, the outcasts, and going so far as to consort even with lepers.

And ironically, he went about threadbare, Francis, the son of the rich cloth merchant Pietro Bernardone, who had previously provided the costliest, and at times, most gaudy clothing and costumes for his profligate son. But now this ungrateful son had actually renounced his father and his patrimony in a histrionic trial before Bishop Guido's court. In front of the bishop and all those standing about, the dramatic Francis had stripped himself of his clothes and placed them at his father's feet—and Bernard watched as Francis then said, "Up till now I have called Pietro Bernardone my father, but now I say, 'Our Father who art in Heaven'"—and Bernard listened.

After that dramatic scene, Francis left town for a while and went to Gubbio where, rumor had it, Francis's friend, Federico Spadalunga, also of a cloth merchant family, gave him something to wear. It was rumored that Francis ministered to lepers outside the walls of Gubbio. And when Francis returned, he spent his time at San Damiano and at the small church of Our Lady of the Angels, which Francis also restored. He called this latter church his Porziuncola, his Little Portion, for it, too, was poor and was located outside the walls of Assisi on the plain below in a swampy area, thickly wooded, near where the leper colonies were.

People thought him mad. He'd not been the same since he returned from a year's imprisonment in Perugia as a prisoner of war. He spent most of his time afterward at home languishing in a deep depression until, as Bernard later learned, Francis had a dream that convinced him to return to battle, to join the papal forces in Apulia under the command of Walter of Brienne. And so, with a few other recruits, Francis set out from Assisi, outfitted with fine armor and a strong young warhorse and a new determination. But after only a day's journey to the city of Spoleto, Francis mysteriously returned to Assisi alone. He rode into town, head bent, no expression on his face, a seeming coward—and Bernard saw and wondered, especially when some said Francis had had another dream in Spoleto and when Francis began to roam aimlessly about the countryside visiting abandoned churches and poor hovels, and Bernard, in the meantime, listened to the rumors and continued to watch and listen, trying to understand what had happened to the young man with so much promise, the young man everyone thought would grow into manhood a leader, a forceful and distinguished citizen of Assisi.

And then something happened—some said it was a vision— in the abandoned ruins of the former wayside church of San Damiano, and Francis began begging stones to repair the rundown church. The people had met his requests for stones with disgust and contempt, but Francis seemed unfazed. He began to smile and sing like someone who'd lost his mind, and that whole developing story led to Francis being brought before the bishop's court and renouncing his father and going off to Gubbio and now returning and continuing the same behavior. He walked through the streets smiling and suddenly breaking into song, praising God. He thanked God aloud, and then thanked his abusers for recognizing what a useless little worm of a man God had chosen to rebuild abandoned churches.

It was then that Bernard began to notice a further change in the manic Francis. He seemed tranquil and at peace no matter how loud the insults became. Francis radiated tranquility even when rocks and garbage were thrown at him as to a mongrel dog who kept interrupting the order and business of the town.

Bernard saw and heard all these things, and like Mary, the Mother of Jesus, he stored them up in his heart, as, day by day, Francis began to seem not a fool, but a saint to Bernard. Or maybe he was a saint and a fool. Whatever, Francis was becoming a happy man, not giddy, but a man whose whole being radiated joy. He had endured hatred and abuse in patience for two years already, and yet his spirit seemed more steadfast with the passing weeks and months and years – and Bernard looked and listened, and then one day he saw. He saw that what was happening to Francis was not madness but a great grace of God—a grace that had begun to draw Bernard himself. He began to see that what was happening was the religious conversion of Francis Bernardone. Bernard remembered the words of the Gospel he'd heard at Mass. The priest said that they were the first words of Jesus. "The time is fulfilled, and the kingdom of God has come near; repent, and believe in the good news" (Mark 1:15).

That is what Bernard had been seeing from afar. Francis was repenting because he believed the kingdom of God had drawn near to him. And that newfound faith had made God's words good news.

But Bernard wanted to be sure. And so he invited Francis to his home for supper, and Francis agreed. Bernard was now near what he had been seeing from afar. And what an easy guest Francis was. The "madman" exhibited the same good cheer and camaraderie he'd been famous for as a teenager and young man. They talked into the night, and Bernard began to see what holiness looks like up close.

When they'd talked themselves out, Bernard asked Francis to stay and told him he'd already had a bed prepared for him in his own room where a lamp burned through the night. Francis readily agreed and when they repaired to the bedroom, Francis threw himself onto the bed and pretended to sleep. Bernard saw that Francis was play acting; he'd always been good at that, so Bernard, too, pretended to sleep and even began to snore, though he was awake and nervously alert should something happen.

And happen it did. When Francis was sure Bernard was sound asleep, he slipped over the side of the bed onto the floor and began to pray. Raising his eyes and hands to heaven, he began to whisper with moving devotion and fervor, "My God and my all." And he kept repeating these words with many tears till dawn. "My God and my all." And no other words.

Bernard listened and watched all night by the light of the lamp, and when dawn came, he sat up and told Francis what had occurred during the night, how he had deceived Francis by pretending he was asleep, how he had been touched by the Holy Spirit while Francis was praying and was inspired to change his life. And then he mustered the courage to say, "Now, Francis, I am determined to renounce the values of this world and follow you who, I am sure, are being led by God."

"Sir Bernard, my spirit is uplifted by your words. They are serious and their consequences difficult. We need to ask guidance of Our Lord Jesus Christ. Let us go, then, to mass and pray afterwards till Terce. Then we will go to the priest and ask him to open the missal for God's advice," which is what they did.

The priest began by making the sign of the cross, then opened the missal three times, the first time to these words that amazed Bernard: "If you wish to be perfect, go, sell your possessions, and give the money to the poor, and you will have treasure in heaven, then come, follow me"(Matthew 19:21). At the second opening, to Bernard's further amazement, they listened to the priest recite Christ's words to his Apostles when he sent them out to preach: "Carry no purse, no bag, no sandals..." (Luke 10:4). It sounded to Bernard that he was listening to what Francis had already been doing. Then the priest opened the missal a third time: "If any want to be my followers, let them deny themselves and take up their cross and follow me" (Matthew 16:24).

To Bernard, and to Francis, too, their mission could not be clearer. These were Christ's words. Bernard had listened and heard. He began to sell all his possessions and, with Francis at his side, he gave the money to the poor. Then with great joy, he joined Francis as they set forth to follow in the footsteps of Christ.

And that was Francis's and Bernard's conversion: making God their all, emptying themselves of possessiveness as Jesus himself did, embracing suffering and pain in peace after the example of Christ, and doing good to others, serving them and giving them the Gospel.

The story of Bernard's conversion is evidently not just a head trip, intellectual knowledge alone. It is knowledge received and acted upon, knowledge of the heart. Something must happen in the heart that changes you because of what you know and have come to believe. Speaking of Francis, Gerard Straub put it this way: "God changed Francis's heart, and his changed heart changed the world." That is what true conversion does, and that is what St. Francis teaches. The knowledge that changes the heart changes you and your interaction with the world, and that new way of knowing and acting changes the world around you and beyond you in space and time.

What, then, does their story mean for us today? What would it look like in practice if we, too, were to hear these words of Jesus? In a talk he gave to the friars, Father Herman Schaluck, the former Minister General of the Friars Minor, spelled out Franciscan faith and action today by opening up for us Jesus's Parable of the Good Samaritan. Jesus tells the story to a lawyer who responded to Jesus's reminder that we are to love God and our neighbor by asking Jesus in return, "And who is my neighbor?" This is how Jesus responds:

A man was going down from Jerusalem to Jericho, and fell into the hands of robbers, who stripped him, beat him, and went away, leaving him half dead. Now by chance a priest was going down that road; and when he saw him, he passed by on the other side. So likewise a Levite, when he came to the place and saw him, passed by on the other side. But a Samaritan while traveling came near him; and when he saw him, he was moved with pity. He went to him and bandaged his wounds, having poured oil and wine on them. Then he put him on his own animal, brought him to an inn, and took care of him. The next day he took out two denarii, gave them to the innkeeper and said, 'Take care of him; and when I come back, I will repay you whatever more you spend.' Which of these three, do you think, was a neighbor to the man who fell into the hands of the robbers? He said, 'The one who showed him mercy.' Jesus said to him, 'Go and do likewise' (Luke 10: 30-38).

Fr. Herman chooses four teachings of the parable that challenge us and show us what rebuilding God's house entails on the personal, practical level. Ultimately, the fruit of conversion is social justice, which is the practical face of what it means to love God and one's neighbor, thereby repairing God's House. It involves, according to Fr. Herman, (1) contemplative seeing, (2) affective response, (3) practical help, and (4) sustained assistance, which are the four movements of the Good Samaritan's story.

There is seeing, and there is seeing. Those who pass by the robbed man fallen by the side of the road, pass by on the "other side." They see but they don't see by consciously moving away from whatever it is that is interrupting what they see as their forward movement. To stop and really look will at least be an inconvenience, and at most a challenge, or even a threat, to their own self-preoccupation, their own selfish comfort and self-importance.

They see and don't see their own intimate connection to the victim of violence. It is not their business or responsibility because they have not prayed that they might have eyes to see. Nor have they practiced contemplation, which is the art of looking intently at something until it begins to look back, forming and informing one's soul. All of creation is interconnected, and the contemplative is one who keeps looking until that connection becomes as real as your connection with those you love deeply and consider beautiful extensions of God. Contemplative prayer enables you to see what is there and to realize your intimate connection to it.

This means that the Samaritan, just like those who passed by, came to the victims' situation with a history. The Samaritan's experience has been such that he sees his connection to the man fallen by the wayside, and he is moved with compassion. His heart responds with brotherly love. His is an affective response. He feels with, which is the root of the word *compassion*, meaning "to suffer with" (Latin, *cum* and *passio*).

If I can no longer feel with, then something has happened to me that makes me so self-referential that even another's tragedy is not my business. It is no concern of mine. Or I am someone who naturally fears becoming involved with anything that could hurt me. Mine it is to take care of myself first and above all others; I am afraid to be hurt by reaching out, and so I have no real practical connection to others, to the world around me, to my own mutual origins with everything God has created. So what could have been a breakthrough encounter, or a growth of love by letting love overcome my fear, puts me instead on the other side of life, the fast lane, or the safe lane, that stops for no one.

Because I have suppressed or denied my own human feeling, I don't feel obliged to help any person or any situation. Someone else will take care of it, someone much more adept at such things than I. The result is a narrowing and eventually a refusing of sensibility. To stay on the side of life with all its messiness and suffering, opens and expands the soul, and I become someone more than a self-referential small person. How large and big must have been the contemplative prayer of little Francis of Assisi that he saw even lepers as his neighbors, and even as his brothers and sisters, whom he must not cross to the other side of the path to avoid.

In fact, Francis not only did not cross to the other side, he was moved to practical help, to bind up their wounds as the Samaritan did; he provided food, he even went among them and, as he said, "worked mercy with them." He became the Good Samaritan of Assisi, providing sustained assistance for them by instructing his brothers to go among the lepers and minister to them if they want to be true Lesser Brothers. By doing so, they would already be Lesser Brothers of Penance, not that being with the lepers was a big penance in the sense of doing penance to subdue their passions, but penance in the sense of repentance, letting God change their vision and their hearts.

Francis himself in that gesture of reaching out to those removed to the margins of society, became Saint Francis, the mirror of the compassionate Christ, who is mirrored in his own parable in the good Samaritan. The compassion of St. Francis was extraordinary, and few there are who can follow him in his heroic charity. But anyone can offer practical help and sustained assistance to the poor and outcast peoples of the world. At least one can do that in the smaller circle of the world he or she lives in. Even a small gesture toward breaking one's own selfish circle to reach out and love those less fortunate begins to expand one's heart and soul.

That is the Franciscan challenge in our own time: contemplative seeing, affective response, practical help, and sustained assistance as *the* way of restoring God's house which is falling into ruins. It is Jesus's own prescription for learning to love. In contemplative prayer we learn to love God who created all things and made them our brothers and sisters. And when we begin to see others for what they are in God's eyes, we are moved to compassion. And when we then reach out to those of our brothers and sisters in distress, the love of God becomes the love of others, all of whom are beloved of God.

In responding, we ourselves become a story, not just an empty shell that hung around for a number of years and then disappeared, leaving behind no story of goodness worth telling because there was no significant act of the will to love our neighbor.

So, repairing God's house is not about stones and mortar as Francis once thought when he heard the voice of Christ. It's about changing our hearts, or rather, letting God change our hearts, a process in which we become fruitful vessels of grace. For it is only repaired hearts that repair the house of God. It is only then that we can fruitfully "Go into the whole world and proclaim the gospel to every creature" (Mark 16:15).

THE WISDOM OF ST. FRANCIS

The Lord has called me into the way of simplicity and humility, and he has indeed made this way known through me and through all those who choose to believe me and follow me. He told me I am to be a new kind of fool in this world.

—*Mirror of Perfection 68*

St. Francis said in a Letter to a Minister (a brother in a position of authority), "Let there be no brother who has sinned, no matter how seriously, who would look into your eyes seeking forgiveness, and go away without it. And should he not seek forgiveness, you should ask him if he wants it. And if after that he were to sin a thousand times, even before your eyes, love him more than me, for this is how you will draw him to the Lord: and always have mercy on such as these."

—Letter to a Minister

I advise, admonish, and exhort you in the Lord Jesus Christ that when you travel through the world you do not quarrel or argue or judge others; rather, be meek, peaceful and modest, courteous and humble, speaking honorably to everyone.

—Rule of 1223, Chapter III

I used to work with my hands, and I still want to, and I want all my brothers to work at a task which is honest and becoming to our manner of life.

Those who do not know how to work should learn, not because they are eager for the pay due their labor, but for example's sake and to banish idleness. And when we receive no pay for our work, let us have recourse to the table of the Lord, begging alms from door to door.

—*The Testament* of St. Francis

.... FIFTH TEACHING ....

Making Peace

Saint Francis shows us just how inseparable the bond is
between concern for nature, justice for the poor, commitment to society, and interior peace.

—Pope Francis, *Laudato Si'*

INTERIOR PEACE IS THE AWARENESS THAT GOD is and dwells in
all of creation, and from that awareness flows the other three
necessary elements of Pope Francis's statement, namely, concern
for nature, justice for the poor, and commitment to society.

All these four are interconnected because God not only is,
but God is the Creator. Everything outside of the inner life of
the Blessed Trinity has its cause in the Trinitarian inter-relating
God: three divine persons whose interrelating love is the energy
that creates a mirror-world outside of itself. The interrelating
love within and among this Trinity of Persons explodes into the
divine energy of creation. We, and the whole universe, are the
children of divine loving. And the three divine persons—Father,
Son, and Holy Spirit—mark everyone and everything that is as
being loved by God. We are loved into existence.

In all creatures, therefore, God is revealed to us: the beauty, the grandeur, the infinite variety, the individuality, and the mystery. That is what St. Francis saw and what he teaches us.

But something has deformed the beauty of God's creation, and that something is injustice. According to St. Bonaventure, in his *Collationes en Hexaëmeron*, "justice makes beautiful what has been deformed." Justice then is the path to peace, peace of mind, peace between and among people, and peace among all God's creatures.

St. Francis, of course, was not a philosopher, a thinker, and theologian like St. Bonaventure. He was a seer, a poet. He spent his whole life trying to see rather than trying to reason things out. He was always looking for signs of God in the world around him. He had found God in the lepers, so he knew that one must look hard and long in order to see the hidden mystery beneath the appearances of things. And because of his deep presence to things and people, he was also a contemplative, one who looks and looks deeply. And that is the first step toward making peace and reconciliation.

Francis looked intently, and he looked with reverence and with love. And as we saw in the previous chapter, this kind of looking elicited an affective response in him, a response of compassion, of feeling with and/or for what is seen. He is moved. And it is that movement of the heart that leads to action. At the very least, it leads to praise; or if what is seen is broken or hurt, it leads to the need to help the other. And that need to help for Francis is not minimal. He pushes the envelope, for example, vis-à-vis the lepers. He doesn't simply give them a coin or food. He goes and lives among them and "works mercy with them." It is a mutual exchange; he works mercy *with* them. They both experience mercy.

That mutual giving and receiving is, I believe, the bedrock of Franciscan peacemaking. By overcoming shame or fear, or whatever it is that is holding you back from reaching out to the poor and broken ones, you enter a startling world of sweetness of soul that is not just self-serving but that accomplishes a profound reconciliation of opposites that makes it possible to experience a new, unexpected bond with the other. And you want to stay there, not necessarily in that physical place but in that spiritual and psychological space where the lion and the lamb lie down together.

Nor is the bond something static. It only endures if you continue to overcome new barriers, cross new and fearsome barriers so that you yourself become the place of reconciliation wherever you go. That kind of portable peacemaker was who St. Francis was.

Pope Francis made such bonding concrete and tangible when he gave *the* sign of what it means to tend the sheep. In his first Holy Week in office, in 2013, he exhorted the priests gathered at the Chrism Mass to be shepherds "living with the smell of the sheep."[8] That is the kind of action peacemaking involves. It is nitty-gritty, hard work, but it also brings with it the sweet fragrance, which we previously thought was a sour and ugly odor.

Crossing borders and overcoming barriers, if done with love, also brings a new vision of reality that enables us to have reverence for everything that is. Francis's early followers used to say that he used to spare lamps, lights, and candles because of the Eternal Light they brought to mind. That is a bit over the top, but that is also who St. Francis was, someone a bit over the top because of how and what he had come to see. His vision was changed so that he could see the light of God radiating from God's creatures, even though he himself, during his last years, was for all practical purposes blind as a result of disease he contracted in Egypt where he went during the Fifth Crusade to try to bring peace and reconciliation between Christians and Muslims.

When he arrived in Damietta in Egypt bringing peace, the Crusaders laughed at him; but the Sultan Malik al-Kamil listened to him, and they became friends, each of them apparently having embraced what they found foreign or even repulsive in the other. That is one of the most dramatic stories from the life of St. Francis, relevant enough today to have merited a docudrama filmed for television as "The Sultan and Saint."

And this is how the story goes. In 1219, in the midst of the Fifth Crusade, Francis went to Damietta, not as a Crusade preacher to cheer on the Crusaders and their supporters, but to preach the Gospel of peace to the Crusader Cardinal Pelagius and to the Sultan, Malik al-Kamil. Then when the Crusaders dismissed him, al-Kamil received him into his camp and spoke with Francis for over two weeks, from September first to the twenty-sixth. The two men recognized in each other a desire for peace and a devotion to their mutual sacred texts, the Gospel of Jesus Christ and the Q'uran. Al-kamil was a devout Suni Muslim, and Francis was, of course, a devout Christian.

Francis had learned early on that God surprises us in unexpected places, like among the lepers, and now in the sultan's camp at the very court of Malik al-Kamil. Francis's daring to make peace with the Muslim forces was a radical departure from the ethos of the day, especially in the Church itself, Pope Innocent himself having called the Fifth Crusade and declared war against Islam for the recapture of the Holy Land for the Church.

Francis, ever obedient to the hierarchical Church, was a faithful preacher and teacher of the decrees of Innocent III's Fourth Lateran Council, especially those relating to moral reforms and the Eucharist. But regarding the Crusade, Francis and his followers are silent of any support. Francis abhorred war, and he had come to see that those we call "the others," even those we consider our enemies, are really our brothers and sisters.

Malik al-Kamil was also a man who desired peace and sued repeatedly for peace but was turned down by the Crusaders, especially under Cardinal Pelagius. When Francis leaves the sultan's camp, al-Kamil gives Francis a beautiful ivory horn that Francis uses later to call people to prayer. He also asks Francis to pray that God will show him (al Kamil) the path.

And when Francis returns to Italy, he adds to his Rule of 1221 these provisions regarding those who go among unbelievers: The brothers can go and live among them as good Christians, and/or if it is God's will, they can preach the Gospel. The phrase, "if it is God's will," is interesting in this context because it echoes the oft-repeated Muslim phrase, *enshallah*, if Allah wills it. These two additions to the Rule may be the origin of the modern saying attributed to St. Francis but which he didn't actually say, namely, "Preach always; if necessary, use words."

Also, in 1224 when Francis goes to La Verna two years before he dies, he takes the Sultan Malik-al-Kamil with him in his heart. He is grieving for al-Kamil and all those Christians and Muslims who will be involved in a new Crusade that Pope Honorius III and Emperor Frederick II are contemplating. The plan is to launch the Crusade in June of 1225. With these thoughts in his mind on La Verna, Francis composes his "Praises of God," which echo Islam's "Ninety-Nine Beautiful Names of God." On the reverse side of the "Praises of God," Francis blesses Brother

Leo and then draws the head of a turbaned man out of whose mouth a large Tau cross emerges, the Tau being Francis's sign of peace in contrast to its symbolism in the Church as the hilt of a Crusader sword. To take up the cross in the Crusade means to take up the sword against the infidels.

Francis proposes the sign of the Tau as a peace symbol, thus once again pushing back against the accepted meaning of the Tau during the Fifth Crusade. Francis sees peace and peacemaking as a way to make beautiful what war and violence have deformed.

The story of Francis and the sultan was possible because of another seminal story of the Franciscan tradition. It is one the friars themselves turn to again and again.

It is winter, and Francis and Leo are on the road returning from Perugia to his beloved Porziuncola, St. Mary of the Angels. The biting cold pierces to the bone, their bodies shaking as they walk. And then, suddenly, as when he was close to despair and Christ spoke to Francis from the cross of San Damiano, Christ now begins to speak through Francis himself out of the cold and bitter silence:

"Brother Leo."

"Yes, father Francis."

"We Lesser Brothers have become examples of holiness and edification for many. But write down, dear brother, that there is no perfect joy in that."

And then Francis is silent, and they walk on in silence, Brother Leo wondering if that is all God has given Francis to say. But again Francis speaks.

"Brother Leo."

"Yes, father Francis."

"We Brothers are known as healers. But even if we were to give sight to the blind, make straight what is crooked, cast out devils, restore hearing to the deaf, make the lame walk and the dumb speak, and raise to life someone who has been dead for days, write down, Brother Leo, that this is not perfect joy."

They are no longer shaking from the cold. They are walking steadily, both of them listening for Christ's words to them.

"Brother Leo."

"Yes, father Francis."

"Should one of the Brothers know every language and every science, and all the Scriptures, so that he could foretell and reveal the future, as well as the secrets of conscience and soul, write down that neither is this perfect joy."

They walk on. Brother Leo wonders if Francis already knows what perfect joy is, or is Christ going to reveal it to them both on the road, as he did to two of his disciples on the road to Emmaus?

"Brother Leo."

"Yes, father Francis. I am listening."

"Brother Leo, little lamb of God, even if one of us Brothers should speak with the tongue of an angel, and would know the courses of the stars and the properties of herbs; and if all the treasures of our sister, Mother Earth, were revealed to him so that he knew the ways of birds, fish, and beasts, of humans, trees, rocks, roots, and waters, write down that neither is this perfect joy."

The walking now has become the prayer of listening in silence, not even the wind or the sound of their steps in the icy mud distracting them from being ears for Christ.

"Brother Leo, even if one of us were such an eloquent preacher that his words could convert unbelievers to faith in Christ, write down that neither is this perfect joy."

Finally, Brother Leo can bear the suspense no longer.

"Father Francis, I beg you in God's name, what then is perfect joy?"

But Francis is silent, waiting for Christ's answer.

"Brother Leo."

"Speak, father Francis. I am listening."

"Brother Leo, when we arrive at St. Mary of the Angels, soaked with rain, stiff with cold, covered with mud, exhausted from hunger, and we knock at the Brothers' door, and the Brother Porter asks angrily, 'Who are you,' and we answer, 'You know us, Brother, we are two of your brothers,' and he says, 'Liars! You are a couple of imposters who wander about deceiving good people and robbing the poor of their alms. Get out of here!'

"And if he refuses to let us in and forces us to stand outside all night in the freezing rain, hungry and shaking from the cold, if we bear such abuse and rejection patiently and calmly without complaint, humbly and charitably thinking that Brother Porter sees us for what we are, and that it is God who moves him to condemn us, then, Brother Leo, gentle lion, write down, 'This is perfect joy.' And if we keep knocking, and he comes out furious and drives us away with abusive words and blows, and we keep bearing all this patiently, cheerfully, and charitably, write down, 'This is perfect joy.'

"And if we return again and again, tearfully begging to be allowed in; and losing all control, our brother comes out with a knotted club and starts beating us, and we keep bearing such abuse patiently and cheerfully, remembering the sufferings of

Christ, the Blessed One, and how he taught us to bear all things for love of him, then write down, Brother Leo, 'This is perfect joy.' For above all the graces that Christ gives his friends is the gift of the Holy Spirit who enables us to conquer self and willingly bear any pain, injury, insult, and hardship for love of Jesus Christ. We cannot glory in any other gift but this because it is not ours but his. That is why the Apostle Paul says, 'May I not boast of anything except the cross of our Lord Jesus Christ…' (Galatians 6: 14).

This story is a favorite among Franciscans. It reveals the source of true Franciscan joy born of humility in imitation of the Poor Crucified Christ. It is what makes a true fraternity a place of healing and forgiveness instead of a place of security, closed to the poor and forsaken, to those who knock uninvited and unwanted at the friary door. In a true fraternity the friars have learned to see their own brokenness, their jealousy, their desire for power. And they have learned to forgive that in themselves and in each other. They learn to laugh at themselves and tell each other that this is perfect joy. Only then does their fraternity become a healing place for others.

And that is why Francis takes Brother Illuminato with him to try to bring Christ's peace to Damietta in the midst of the Fifth Crusade, two brothers with no illusions about themselves going where they know ahead of time that perfect joy is waiting for them. And this is how it came to pass that two Lesser Brothers entered and were accepted, after much infliction of perfect joy from the Crusaders and the sultan's guards, into the presence of Sultan Malik al-Kamil.

This is the way peacemaking happens. This is what St. Francis says in word and deed.

THE WISDOM OF ST. FRANCIS

St. Francis used to say to his brothers, "Go, announce peace to all people; preach repentance for the remission of sins. Be patient in trials, watchful in prayer, and steadfast in weariness. Be modest in speech, responsible in your actions, and grateful to your benefactors. And in return an eternal kingdom is being made ready for you."
—St. Bonaventure, *Major Life of St. Francis*: *3.7*

The peace, which you proclaim with words, must dwell even more abundantly in your hearts. Do not provoke others to anger or give scandal. Rather, let your gentleness draw them to peace, goodness, and concord. This is our vocation: to heal wounds, to bind what is broken, to bring home those who are lost.
—*Legend of the Three Companions, 58*

SIXTH TEACHING

God's House Is All of Creation

As HE LOOKED OUT OF HIS CAVE and down to Assisi from the heights of Mount Subasio, it was as if the whole of creation were spread out beneath his cave, and God's goodness rushed in upon him. He could only think of that pure Goodness and how God shares his life with us. Everything good and beautiful comes from God. God went so far as to give us one of the persons of the Blessed Trinity, Jesus the Christ, who came among us as Jesus, the carpenter's son from Nazareth. Jesus was one of us, and yet he was more. He came to show us how to praise God, though only he could praise God perfectly. Only Jesus was the perfect lover of God outside the circle of the Blessed Trinity. Everything and everyone comes from the Trinity, including Jesus. And everything that is exists in Jesus Christ.

This was beyond Francis's thinking. These were thoughts too high for him, a merchant's son who understood the give-and-take that is business. The world of business Francis knew, and he knew that God's economy was different. All the supply was on God's side. All we could give in return was praise through Jesus Christ, who alone can give back adequately what the Father gives eternally. Praise we can give. And care for and of all God has created outside the Trinity, beginning with Jesus himself who sums up and contains all of creation in his own divine nature.

Francis knew the two stories of the beginnings of things in the book of Genesis. One story emphasizes human beings' dominion over all lesser creatures. The other story was about humans' care and nurturing of all creatures, including Earth itself. Francis loved the second story more. It appealed to who he was and how he saw his relationship to the world around him. So, he would praise God through Jesus Christ with all creatures, for all creatures, and in and by means of all creatures. And he would care for them and nourish them, as God's words in Genesis said he should. That is an economy Francis could understand: God gives all good; humans in return praise and care. He knew he had to praise or he wouldn't be able to care and nourish. And he had to care and nourish or his praise would be empty. That was to be his story. That was everyone's deepest story. Bad things would befall us all, but praise and care would keep us going. And that was love, to praise and care for, no matter what. That's what God's good merchant does: receive good unlimited and pay it back with praise and care. That was the economy of love that was the counter weight to the economy of money that was beginning to make its way into Assisi.

And so he would always keep praise in the forefront of his and his brothers' lives. They would all try to remember to praise. And to help them he will direct the brother gardener to not plant the whole garden with food plants, but to set aside a plot for those plants, which in their season would bloom with Brother Flowers. Then when the brothers saw the pretty little flower bed with its sweetly scented herbs and flowering plants it would invite everyone to praise God; for Brother Flowers will say, "God made me for you, O human!"

Thursday, July 13, 2017, *The New York Times*: "A chunk of floating ice roughly the size of Delaware broke away from the Antarctica Peninsula this week, NASA confirmed on Wednesday, producing one of the largest icebergs ever recorded and providing a glimpse of how the Antarctic ice sheet might ultimately start to fall apart."

I felt a shiver run up my arms as I held the paper. "O humans!" I cried out to the empty room. I wondered were we in any way responsible for accelerating such an alarming change of the planet. What would this mean? My mind raced to St. Francis's, "Canticle of the Creatures," to the stanza on our sister Mother Earth, who "sustains and directs us, / bringing forth all kinds of fruits / with colored flowers and herbs." And the flowers and herbs cried out, "God made us for you, O humans!"

The original Umbrian language for what our sister Mother Earth does reads, "*laquale ne sustenta et governa*," literally "who sustains and governs," rendered in one translation as "In her sovereignty (*governa*) she nourishes (*sustenta*)." But in the Italian language *governa* also means "to look after, to direct and care for." St. Francis sees the earth as the gift of God through which God looks after us, cares for us, letting Earth direct us (*governa*) and sustains (*sustenta*) our lives. What then is our response to such a gift?

It is surely not indifference, or worse, dismissal! And what then are the consequences if we not only dismiss but abuse her who is our sister, Mother Earth, God's gift to sustain and nourish us? And what kind of arrogance and greed abuses Earth instead? It makes one weep and be tempted to hate those who rape Earth, were it not for the knowledge that hate diminishes the effects of God's love and care even more. We've had enough of hate and neglect that creates such scenes as these from William Blake's poem "London."

> How the chimney-sweeper's cry
> Every black'ning church appals;
> And the hapless soldier's sigh
> Runs in blood down palace walls.[9]

War and greed and neglect. How they mirror one another, even now eight hundred years after St. Francis sang his "Canticle of the Creatures" and two hundred years after Blake's poem!

I felt helpless to figure out how we might turn our lives around and reverence our Sister Mother Earth again, and let her take care of us and nourish us in the face of what, in the words of Blake's, "The Tyger," is behind the tiger's fearsome eyes:

> In what distant deeps or skies
> Burnt the fire of thine eyes?
> On what wings dare we aspire?
> What the hand dare seize the fire?[10]

Something ominous is beginning to happen. How much of it is of our own making? Perhaps once again St. Francis can help us.

His greatest teaching, in his words and in his life, is that God is. He had experienced the "absence" of the one Jesus called, "Our Father." And that same Father had found the lost Francis through God's presence in other human beings, especially in the lowliest and most rejected, like the lepers.

After his imprisonment in Perugia and after his long recuperation afterward at home in Assisi, the natural world, too, seemed dead, the glory of its charm no longer real to Francis, but then the same God found Francis there, too. Once he had come to know and remember that there is a God dwelling among us and within us, then nature also began to speak to him of God. As Brother Thomas of Celano, Francis's first biographer, wrote,

> St. Francis praised the Artist in every one of his works; whatever he found in things made, he referred to their Maker. He rejoiced in all the works of the Lord's hands, and with joyful vision saw into the reason and cause that gave them life. In beautiful things he came to know Beauty itself. To him all things were good. They cried out to him, "He who made us is infinitely good." By tracing His footprints in things, Francis followed the Beloved wherever He led. He made from created things, a ladder to His throne.[11]

St. Francis had an intuitive grasp of the infinite chasm between the creature and the Creator. And in Jesus Christ he saw the Creator bridging that chasm to be one like us. Francis's whole life, after his conversion, was to respond by his life and actions to so profound a self-emptying by God, the eternal Creator of all things. He does this by praising and thanking God for the work of God's hands, by reverencing every created thing, and by emptying himself of everything he clings to that keeps him from meeting the God who became Incarnate out of pure, selfless love for us.

Francis, according to his first companions, used to weep profusely and spontaneously. And when they asked him why he wept so, Francis answered, "Because Love is not loved." That response is why Francis loved creatures so deeply. Everything in

God's creation exists because God made it in love and proved that love by becoming one with creation in the mystery of the Incarnation. And that is why

> Francis had a great affection even for worms because of what Psalm 21 said of the suffering Savior: "I am a worm and not a man." He used to pick them up when he saw them along the road and put them in a safe place where no one would walk on them. And in winter he would be concerned about the bees that they might die of the cold, so he would prepare honey or the best wine for them. He was moved and fascinated by the working of bees and would often spend a day in prayer praising them and other industrious creatures of the Lord. In fact, filled with the Spirit of God, as Francis was, he did not cease to glorify, praise and bless the Creator and Lord of all in all God's elements and creatures.
>
> The beauty of flowers, too, brought him great delight in their shape and color and sweet fragrance that lifted his heart and soul to him who is the Root of Jesse. And when he came upon a field of flowers, he would preach to them as if they could actually understand him, and he would invite them to praise God. He often did the same in fields of grain, in vineyards, in the woods and among the beautiful things of all fields, fountains of water and the green things of gardens, earth and fire, air and wind, all the while calling on them to love the Lord and serve him! It was as if he had already attained that freedom of the glory of the children of God that St. Paul wrote of in his Letter to the Romans, "There is therefore now no condemnation for those who are in Christ Jesus" (Romans 8:1).[12]

Creation, as the out-of-doors, or nature, is the place of freedom where the laws are based on relationship instead of ownership, of nurturing rather than overpowering and subduing. It is more the place of Trinitarian relating than hierarchical relating, of openings rather than closings. As the Jesuit poet Gerard Manley Hopkins says in his poem "God's Grandeur": "There lives the dearest freshness deep down things."[13] Francis first realized this truth in his meeting with Christ in the lepers. If God could dwell in someone who seemed repulsive to the young Francis, someone whom others rejected, then God could dwell and be present to us in a poor carpenter's son from Nazareth.

Further meditation convinced Francis that God indwells everything God has created; therefore, nothing is evil in itself, and everything is worthy of reverence and respect because of its Creator. And further, every creature is made holy in the mystery of God's presence among us in Jesus. Jesus sanctified all of creation by becoming, though he was God, one with creatures and among creatures, animate and inanimate.

This insight of Francis was spelled out and opened up by the great medieval Franciscan philosopher/theologian, Blessed John Duns Scotus. He named this insight the Absolute Predestination and Universal Primacy of Christ, a rather intimidating phrase; but basically it means that Duns Scotus rejected the prevalent teaching of the time that the Incarnation was the result of the sin of Adam, that Jesus came because Adam sinned, and we needed saving. Duns Scotus rejected this thinking because he found it inconceivable that the Incarnation should be dependent upon something as negative as sin. He writes:

> I say then that the Fall was not the reason of Christ's predestination. Even if no angel had fallen, nor any

human, Christ would still have been predestined—yes,
even if no others were to have been created save only
Christ.[14]

These words of Duns Scotus establish Christ as the pinnacle of
creation, containing in himself the patterns of everything that is
created and as the primary intention of God in communicating
God's perfections. Gerard Manley Hopkins, who was deeply
influenced by Duns Scotus, states in his spiritual writings, "The
first intention of God outside himself, or as they say, *ad extra*
(outwards), the first outstress of God's power, was Christ" (S,
197). Simply put, this means that Christ is willed by the Trinity
for all eternity out of love, independent of sin and redemption.

So, for Duns Scotus the Incarnation is an act of love that would
have taken place in one form or another whether or not there
had been any sin. As Franciscan scholar Fr. Alan Wolter put it
in one of his lectures, "God as God could not perform the act of
an inferior nature; so from all eternity God willed to become a
creature in order to express that aspect of God's love which was
impossible for God alone, namely to love Himself from within
His creation."

Duns Scotus argues that Christ is first in God's intentions. It
is Christ who is infinitely able to render to God supreme glory
and perfect love. Christ is the first to be conceived in the mind of
the Creator in projecting a creative plan. Christ is willed freely
and lovingly in God, not as an improvisation or second guess
merely to repair a sinful breach. As St. Paul puts it in Colossians
1:15–20:

He is the image of the invisible God, the firstborn of all
creation; for in him all things in heaven and on earth were

created, things visible and invisible, whether thrones or dominions or rulers or powers—all things have been created through him and for him. He himself is before all things, and in him all things hold together. He is the head of the body, the church; he is the beginning, the firstborn from the dead, so that he might come to have first place in everything. For in him all the fullness of God was pleased to dwell, and through him God was pleased to reconcile to himself all things, whether on earth or in heaven, by making peace through the blood of his cross.

It is, then, because Christ was the perfect adorer of God, the perfect bridge between creatures and the Creator, that he could even bridge the gap created by sin. Sin was not first in God's intention, but because we sinned, when God comes among us, Christ's perfect adoration is his perfect sacrifice. He didn't come to repair sin; he came to be the firstborn perfect creature; but because we sinned, Christ showed us just how great is God's love: God not only becomes one of us, but he dies with us and for us and makes peace by his death on the cross.

St. Francis was keenly aware that Christ is the firstborn of *all* creatures, not only humans. And so we have many stories of Francis and animals in Franciscan tradition.

In the late days when the brothers seemed to no longer listen to his admonitions and Gospel teaching and when he felt distant from those brothers who were changing the way of life Christ had given them, Francis would go up a mountain or into the woods and preach to the animals. And they would come to him and seem to be listening—at least they were silent—and small, vulnerable animals or birds, especially, would sit in his lap or light on his shoulders. They felt safe there, as he did with them.

One time, near the brothers' place of solitude at Greccio, a brother brought him a young hare that had been freed from a trap. He immediately felt compassion for the hare and said, as though he were addressing one of the brothers, "Brother Hare, why did you let yourself get caught?" And the hare tried to wriggle out of the hands of the brother who then let it go to Francis. It leapt into his lap and, no longer cowering, relaxed as in its warren with its own mother.

Francis felt affection for the little creature and stroked it as a mother would. Then he placed the leveret on the ground. But it immediately leapt back into his lap again and again, until Francis asked the brother who'd found the trapped hare to take him deep into the nearby woods where he returned to the world of nature, which is both refuge and danger.

Maybe that is what Francis must do with his brothers: Let them come to him as to a mother and then release them, free them to enter the world of their Rule of Life where they were no longer controlled by him but free to choose the Rule, which was their refuge from traps the world would inevitably lay for them.

Their own consciences and their Rule. They were their guides through the woods where both refuge and danger lay. Conscience and Rule would show them how to love every creature of the woods as their brother or sister without being trapped by loving the creature more than the Creator whose love is infinite and everlasting and who spent time among us as a human being.

Francis had been in the dark wood of the world, which was mostly inside his own mind; and then the Lord spoke to him in dream and outside of dream, and what seemed dark and forbidding before was turned into a light that overcame the dark. And that Light is Christ. Conscience and Rule would hold on to the light, even with the dark trying to overcome it. And that Light illumines everything created and makes it good, for the Light that is Christ shines brighter than a mother's love.

That is why he loved all creatures. He knew where they came from and who sustains them. How then can we abuse or neglect such signs and presences of the living God? To do so would be the deadliest of sins, for it would separate us from the sign of the presence of God among us, namely, everything that God has made.

"Brothers," he wanted to cry out, "hold on to the Rule and your Conscience. Your conscience will lead you back to God; the Rule will lead you to the Gospel where Christ, who is the Way, the Truth, and the Life, shows us who we and all creatures are, children of the Light that shines in the dark."

There is a terrifying scene in Ignazio Silone's great novel, *Bread and Wine*, in which Cristina, having read Pietro Spina's diary and realizing he is not a priest but a fugitive communist in disguise being pursued by the fascist police and that he loves her, decides to pursue him into the mountains of Abruzzi in a snow storm. Exhausted and blinded by the blowing snow, she keeps calling his name until she collapses into the deep snow:

> And every so often she went on calling, 'Pietro, Pietro.' Eventually a voice in the distance answered her, but it was not a human voice. It was like the howling of a dog, but it was sharper and more prolonged. Cristina probably recognized it. It was the howl of a wolf. The howl of prey. The summons to other wolves scattered around the mountain. The invitation to the feast. Through the

driving snow and the darkness of approaching night Cristina saw a wild beast coming toward her, quickly appearing and disappearing in the dips and rises in the snow. She saw others appear in the distance. She knelt, closed her eyes, and made the sign of the cross.[15]

The first time I read that shattering ending, I thought of the story of the wolf of Gubbio and how Francis was able to tame this lone wolf. I wondered, why was the wolf alone? Was he the alpha wolf who, once he had found prey, would howl for the alpha female and for the rest of the pack, which is usually the offspring of the two alpha wolves? Or were the other wolves dead and he alone remained, or had he been separated from the others somehow and ended up outside the town of Gubbio terrorizing the citizens of the town? Whatever the case may be, the story of Francis and the wolf of Gubbio ends up in *The Little Flowers of St. Francis*, which was written around 1330, late in the sources of the life of St. Francis, who died in 1226. Neither the first biography of St. Francis by Brother Thomas of Celano that appeared in 1229 nor Thomas of Celano's second biography that appeared in 1247 contains this story of the wolf of Gubbio. The first clear reference to the story appears for the first time around 1290 in the Versified Life of St. Francis by the French poet Henri d'Avranches. A hint of the story appears in a mid-thirteenth century chronicle of the Benedictine Monastery of San Verecondo at Vellingegno between Gubbio and Perugia:

Late one evening while Francis was riding on a donkey along the San Verecondo road with a companion, wearing a coarse sack over his shoulders, some farm workers called to him, saying, 'Brother Francis, stay with us and don't go farther, because some fierce wolves are running around here, and they will devour your donkey and hurt you, too.'

Then St. Francis said: 'I have not done any harm to Brother Wolf that he should dare devour our Brother Donkey. Good-by, my sons. And fear God.'

So St. Francis went on his way. And he was not hurt.

A farmer who was present told us this.[16]

Despite the relatively late date of the full story of the wolf of Gubbio, there is something archetypal about this story, something that is inside and outside of human beings. Furthermore, wolves have been common in Italy for years and years. As late as 1956 packs of starving wolves were once again terrorizing villagers in central Italy. Those who are poor and vulnerable fear wolves, whether they are threatening their animals and children, or are not wolves at all, but ravenous humans who devour their livelihood and threaten them with pain and suffering if they don't hand over most of what they are able to produce to these "wolves in sheep's clothing" who own the land or pay them hardly anything for their crops.

Enter St. Francis in the mythology of the poor. He tames the wolf; he talks to him like a brother, even calling him, "Brother Wolf." He assures the townspeople of Gubbio that the wolf will not harm them ever again if they provide enough food for him to eat. Something has been restored, a sort of paradise where the lamb and the wolf lie down together in peace. Something deformed has been made beautiful again through a sort of social contract between the animal world and the human world, between the haves and the have nots. All of those elements are contained in this fairy tale where everyone lives happily ever after. That is why the story is in *The Little Flowers of St. Francis*, a book which is one of the classics of Western Literature. And I include this story in this book about the teachings of St. Francis because so much of Franciscan spirituality is passed down to us in stories. Franciscan spirituality is story spirituality, not a methodology, and so in conclusion I pass on one of the great stories of the Franciscan tradition, a story that typifies why St. Francis is the Patron Saint of Peacemakers and of Animals, why he is pictured in art again and again talking to and listening to the animals. Here is my retelling of this precious story based on Raphael Brown's modern translation of the text medieval friars handed down to us.

Once when St. Francis was staying in Gubbio, something marvelous happened that made him famous among the people there.

In the countryside near Gubbio there was a large and fierce wolf that was so famished that it had been killing not only animals but human beings, too. The citizens of Gubbio were living in terror because the wolf often stalked those coming out of the city gates. They'd begun to carry weapons when they went out into the country, just as if they were going to war. But their weapons proved useless when the wolf surprised them on their way and they found themselves face to face with its ravenous mouth. And so they began to be afraid to leave the town.

Then God, wishing to show the citizens of Gubbio the holiness of St. Francis, moved the saint to go as God's messenger and meet the wolf. But when St. Francis told the people what God had told him to do, they protested saying, "Brother Francis, Beware! Don't go outside the gate. Some armed citizens have tried to confront the wolf, and they never returned. He'll surely kill you, Brother Francis, poor unarmed beggar that you are. He'll bare his sharp teeth and attack you."

But St. Francis had already put his hope in Jesus Christ who is Lord of all creatures. And so it was that St. Francis, armed only with the sign of the cross, strode bravely out of the town with one of his brothers. He told his companion that all they needed to do was to put their faith and trust in the Lord who said that those who believe in him would walk among asps and basilisks and even among wolves or lions or dragons. And with that the two of them strode forth to meet the wolf.

Then some peasants who were following hesitantly some distance behind stopped and said, "Brother Francis, we can't go any farther; this is too dangerous."

"Okay," St. Francis said. "Wait here. And you, too, brother. I'm going alone now to the wolf's lair."

Just then, in the sight of the people who were standing on the city wall watching, the wolf came rushing, its large mouth open, right toward Francis and his companion.

But St. Francis stood still and unflinching and made the sign of the cross over the wolf. And the power of God, flowing now not only from St. Francis but from his companion brother, as well, checked the wolf in his tracks, and it suddenly closed its ravenous mouth and began to slow down to a walk.

Then St. Francis called to the wolf: "Come to me, Brother Wolf. In the name of Christ I command you not to hurt me or my brother or anyone else."

And, marvelous to tell, the wolf lowered its head and lay down like a meek lamb at the feet of St. Francis who said gently but firmly, "O Brother Wolf, Brother Wolf, you've done great harm in this region, and you've committed horrible crimes by killing your fellow creatures without mercy. You've been killing not only your fellow animals but humans, too, who are created in the image of God. You deserve to be put to death like the worst thief and murderer. And right now the whole town is your enemy. But, my brother, God wants me to make peace between you and them so that you won't harm them anymore, and they will in turn forgive you all your past deeds, so that neither humans nor dogs will hunt you down ever again."

The wolf showed it agreed with this plan by wagging not only its tail but its whole body and by nodding its head.

Then St. Francis spoke again: "Good Brother Wolf, since you are willing to keep this peace pact, I promise you the people of Gubbio will feed you every day for as long as you live. You will never again suffer hunger so great that you will be tempted to kill or maim to satisfy your hunger. But I need your promise, Brother Wolf, that in return for this favor you will never again harm any animal or human. Can you promise me that?"

And the wolf nodded its head as a promise.

But St. Francis said, "I need a further sign and pledge that you will keep your promise." And St. Francis held out his hand.

The wolf then raised its front paw and gently placed it in St. Francis's open palm as a sign of its pledge to keep its promise.

Then St. Francis said, "Now, Brother Wolf, in the name of Jesus Christ, come with me into the town and have no fear because the people will now make their peace with you and give you their pledge."

And they walked in together, the wolf at St. Francis's side padding along as gentle as a lamb.

The news of this sight spread quickly so that the whole town began to assemble in the market place to see this amazing work of God's saint.

And when they had all come together, St. Francis began to preach to them, among other things, of how this calamity befell them because of their sins. And they should fear the pains of hell even more than they feared the wolf who could only kill their bodies.

"So, dear people of Gubbio, come back to the Lord and do penance for your sins, and God will free you from the wolf in this world and from hell in the next world."

Then he added, "Listen, everybody! Brother Wolf who is standing here among us has given me his pledge to live in peace with you and never hurt you if you promise to feed him every day. And I pledge myself as guarantor of this pact between you."

Then all the people spoke in a loud voice promising and pledging to feed Brother Wolf. And St. Francis turned to the wolf and said, "And you, Brother Wolf, do you promise to keep your pledge not to hurt any animal or human being?"

The wolf then knelt down and, bowing its head, wagged again its whole body and wiggled its ears to show he would keep his part of the bargain.

But St. Francis, wanting to assure the people, said, "Brother Wolf, you gave me your pledge outside the gate. Now I want you to give it again in front of all these good people."

And Brother Wolf once again raised its paw and placed it in the hand of St. Francis.

Then all the people rejoiced and gave thanks to God for sending St. Francis to them to make peace between them and the wolf and to restore the joy and tranquility of their town.

And so it happened that from that day forward the wolf and the citizens of Gubbio kept their pledge to one another.

The wolf lived two more years, going from door to door when it was hungry. And they say that not a single dog barked at Brother Wolf.

And when their wolf finally died, the people were sorry and sad because they'd grown to love their Brother Wolf with his peaceful kindness and patience and because he reminded them of the holiness and virtues of St. Francis whose intercession with God worked so great a miracle in their town.

Praised be our Lord and Savior, Jesus Christ. Amen.

Years ago when I first read this story it struck me that it worked as both a miracle story and an allegorical story. I asked myself, "Could the wolf symbolize something inside of us that we need to attend to and make peace with?" And the answer came in writing this paragraph in my first book, *Francis: The Journey and the Dream*:

> As soon as he had heard the news of the wolf of Gubbio, Francis felt sympathy for the wolf. There was something of the wolf in all of nature, that ravenous hunger, that restless pursuit, that baring of the fangs, so symbolic of what was wild and violent in all of us. But he saw in the wolf not so much the stalker as the stalked. Everyone feared wolves and disliked them, and he saw in the eyes of wolves a fear, a hunted look, an anger and hostility that wanted to devour everything in sight in order to avenge their own hurt and alienation. Wolves, after all, were like people. If you feared them and ostracized them and excluded them, they eventually turned into what you were afraid they were anyway.[17]

Looking back almost fifty years, that passage seems prophetic of what is happening in the world today. There is, it seems to me, room for lots of tending to our inner wolf.

THE WISDOM OF ST. FRANCIS

Francis embraced all things with an unheard of love and

devotion, speaking to them of the Lord and exhorting them to praise Him.

—Thomas of Celano, *Second Life of St. Francis,* 165

His was an extraordinary meekness, not only toward other people, but also toward animals. He called all animals 'brother' or 'sister' and we read in the story of his life how even wild animals came running to him as their friend and companion.

—From a sermon of St. Bonaventure, October 4, 1255

It happened once, when St. Francis was preaching in Aviano, that he could not be heard because of the chattering of a flock of swallows building their nests there. So St. Francis said to the birds:

'My Sister Swallows, you have had your say. It is now my turn to speak. Be quiet now and listen to the word of the Lord.'

Then to the astonishment of the people standing about, the little birds fell silent and did not move until St. Francis finished preaching.

—Thomas of Celano, *First Life of St. Francis,* 59

Once St. Francis was sitting in a boat near a port in the lake of Rieti. A fisherman who had just caught a large carp rowed over to the saint and kindly offered him the fish. St. Francis accepted it joyfully and gracefully, and immediately began calling it "Brother." Then he placed the fish gently in the water and began praising the name of the Lord. But all the while Francis prayed, the fish continued to play beside the boat and would not leave until St. Francis finished his prayer and gave it permission to leave.

And so it was that St. Francis's total obedience to God gave him great dignity before creatures, who in turn obeyed him.

—Thomas of Celano, *First Life of St. Francis*, 61

All-powerful, most holy, most high and supreme God,
Holy and just Father,
Lord, King of heaven and earth,
we thank you for yourself
for through your holy will
and through your Son
with the Holy Spirit,
You have created all things spiritual and corporal
and having made us in your own image and likeness,
You placed us in paradise.

—Rule of 1221, Chapter XXIII

At dawn, when the sun rises, everyone should praise God who has created Brother Sun for our service, for through him our eyes light up the day; in the evening, when night descends, everyone should praise God through Brother Fire, for through him our eyes light up the night. We are all, as it were, blind, and it is through these two brothers that the Lord gives light to our eyes. We should praise the Lord, then, in a special way for these creatures and for the others, too, who serve us day by day.

—*Mirror of Perfection*, 119

CHAPTER | *seven*

SEVENTH TEACHING

The Joy of Humble Praise and Service of God

A human being is part of the whole, called by us, "Universe," a part limited in time and space. He experiences himself, his thoughts and feelings as something separated from the rest—a kind of optical delusion of his consciousness. The striving to free oneself from this delusion is the one issue of true religion. Not to nourish the delusion but to try to overcome it is the way to reach the attainable measure of peace of mind.

> —Albert Einstein in a typed letter to Dr. Robert S. Marcus, February 12, 1950.

TWO YEARS BEFORE FRANCIS DIED, HE WAS granted the grace of seeing the whole picture, as it were, instead of just the piecemeal picture of his own world, the world of himself and his followers, the people he met along the way, the concerns of his own small world. Physics must become first a sort of metaphysics. As the twentieth-century physicist David Bohm once put it, "We must turn physics around; instead of starting with parts and showing

83

how they relate, we must start with the whole." That is the vision God gave to St. Francis toward the end of his life and this is how we know that.

After he had received the sacred stigmata in 1224, two years before he died, Francis returned to Assisi. But he did not go to his beloved Porziuncola, St. Mary of the Angels, but to San Damiano where Clare and her Sisters lived and where he had heard the voice of Christ from the cross saying, "Francis, go and repair my church which as you see is falling into ruins." That is what he had tried to do, his life on earth now coming to an end.

He was, for all practical purposes, blind from the trachoma that he had contracted in Damietta, Egypt during his sojourn there in the midst of the Fifth Crusade. He was hemorrhaging, as well, from the wounds of Christ. He was so weak he lay in torment for over fifty days in a small lean-to beside the monastery of the nuns of San Damiano, with field mice running over his emaciated body. Imprisoned as he was in his own body, how terrible the memories of his imprisonment in Perugia must have been! He was deeply depressed by the direction some of the Brothers were going in, seeming to him to have abandoned Lady Poverty.

Then, when he was at his deepest point of near despair, the Voice and a vision once more graced his waning life.

Darkness again. And pain. This time it is his eyes. They pain him so deeply that he cannot rest, cannot sleep or pray. Again he is in prison, and he is afraid, even here in this small lean-to beside San Damiano that Clare and the other Poor Ladies have prepared for him.

He is so tired. It is only a month or so now since he'd returned to the Umbrian Valley after the long, painful journey from La

Verna. He can no longer walk. He'd had to ride a donkey from La Verna because of the pain of the nails in his feet, the nails of Christ's passion. Nails, too, in his hands, and a wound in his side. All were love-gifts from his Beloved—Jesus, his Lord and God.

Added to these burdens, he is depressed, not because of pain, or his blind eyes, which cannot bear the light of the sun by day or even a candle by night without hemorrhaging. That pain he can endure. But the further suffering that depresses him comes from the direction the brothers are now taking the Fraternity. They are building houses, contrary to the Rule, and they seem to be constantly acquiring more books, as if Salvation comes from books and the knowledge they give us. In all this they are abandoning Lady Poverty, as well as the one knowledge that matters, the knowledge of Jesus Christ.

And now, too, as in that terrible Perugian imprisonment, he cannot rest because field mice have been crawling over his body, and he in darkness, his memory enlarging and exaggerating what he cannot see.

He bleeds in soul and body. And this night is almost too much to bear. He cries out to the Lord, "Help me, O Lord, with this pain and suffering. Help me to bear it patiently!"

And the Lord hears him. Francis hears the Voice again in the depths of his soul.

"Francis, my brother, hear my voice. If the whole of the earth and the fabric of the universe were to turn to pure gold and rocks and pebbles turned to gems, and your pain were taken away, and then in addition to this, and as a reward for all your pain and suffering, you were given a treasure so precious that even gold and precious gems would not be worth mentioning in comparison, wouldn't you rejoice and gladly bear what you are now bearing?"

"Oh, yes, Lord. I would be happy and filled with joy and rejoice with all my soul!"

"Then, Francis, rejoice and be happy. Your illness and suffering is the pledge, the promise of my kingdom. By merit of your patience and long-suffering, you can be firm and secure that you are in my kingdom."

This story is the reason Francis decided to sing "The Canticle of the Creatures," which contains the seventh teaching of St. Francis. For the next morning, the Voice now silent, Francis told the brothers what happened and then said, "Therefore for God's glory, for my consolation, and the edification of others, I want to compose a new "Praises of the Lord" for all God's creatures. Daily we fail to appreciate so great a blessing by not praising as we should the Creator and dispenser of all these gifts." He sat down, concentrated, then began to sing:

> Most High, all-powerful, good Lord,
> yours is the praise,
> the glory and the honor
> and every blessing.
>
> To you alone, Most High,
> do they belong,
> and no one is worthy
> to speak your name.
> Praised be you, my Lord
> with all your creatures,
> especially Sir Brother Sun,
> who is the day through whom
> you bring us light.

And he is lovely, shining
with great splendor,
for he heralds you, Most High.

Praised be you, my Lord,
through Sister Moon and Stars.
In heaven have you formed them,
lightsome and precious and fair.

Praised be you, my Lord,
through Brother Wind, through
air and cloud, through calm
and every weather by which
you sustain your creatures.

Praised be you, my Lord,
through Sister Water,
so very useful and humble,
precious and chaste.

Praised be you, my Lord
through Brother Fire,
by whom you light up
the night, and he is
handsome and merry,
robust and strong.

Praised be you, My Lord,
through our Sister, Mother Earth,
who sustains and directs us
bringing forth all kinds of fruits
and colored flowers and herbs.

Praised be you, my Lord,
through those who forgive
for your love
and who bear sickness and trial.

Blessed are those
who endure in peace,
for by you, Most High,
they will be crowned.

Praised be you, my Lord,
through our Sister Bodily Death
from whom no living being
can escape.

How dreadful for those
who die in mortal sin!
How blessed are those she
finds in your most holy will
for the second death
can do them no harm.

O praise and bless my Lord,
thank him and serve him
humbly but grandly!

In one sense, what the Voice said to Francis is what Francis already knew, that beneath what appears on the surface is the priceless gold of what everything really is: God's precious creation. And even greater than the created thing is its re-creation in eternity. Everything will be a new heaven and a new earth and it is struggling to be so even now. Humans who join in the sufferings, the birth-pangs, of all creation become transformed through their patience and long suffering and see at once that God's future kingdom is already being realized in and with them. For everything suffers change, and only human beings who are able to see and understand can embrace that change willingly even when it involves darkness and suffering.

What Francis had come to believe about all of this, and especially about the interconnectedness of the whole universe, he now knows with certitude because of the vision given to him in his dark cell of suffering at San Damiano. And this revelation, this voice, gives him a way to express it, namely through a canticle, a sung poem of praise of God through, with, in, for, and by means of God's creatures, who have become Francis's brothers and sisters, animate and inanimate.

And so he tells his brothers that he is going to sing a *new* song of praise of God in whose kingdom we already dwell, and whose perfection will be revealed when we embrace our Sister Bodily Death, and she finds us living in God's most holy will.

Francis answered God's revelatory voice by saying he would happily embrace his sufferings and pain, knowing now for certain that they will be the pledge of entering God's kingdom of painless, perfect interconnectedness between and among all created things.

Francis knew this was true by means of a lifetime of learning how to live with all creatures, loving them and serving them, and giving God thanks for them. And now, two years before he will embrace Sister Death, God assures Francis and us that everything belongs to everything else, and everything belongs to God. So everything is thereby holy and worthy of care, and reverence, and a song of God's praise.

Francis now knows how to express what he had known for years but didn't know he knew until he heard God's voice and began to sing, each word showing what he didn't know he knew. And that song gave him great joy in the composing and in the singing, for God is. And to serve and sing God is to live forever.

But if we think that singing and serving creatures alone brings joy, Francis reminds us that "singing joy" comes out of that other joy that he calls "Perfect Joy," and which comes from loving and serving the Poor Crucified Christ, which is another story of the love that made all the other loves possible.

As a young man recovering from war in a kind of post-traumatic haze, he had fallen in love with Jesus and his Gospel of love. And he remained all his life in that love, suffering from seeing Christ rejected and dying again in Francis's own time. Even some of his own brothers seemed to Francis Judas-like in their betrayal of the Poor Christ who was *the* revelation of God's love, entering his own creation out of utter love for us. Francis helped resurrect the Christ of the Gospels who showed Francis the way that alone would renew the earth and all life that dwells upon it.

"Go and repair my house," Jesus says to Francis as he prayed before the San Damiano Crucifix. "Go and repair my house which, as you see, is falling into ruins." He not only repaired the little house of San Damiano, but the larger house where God dwells, Earth itself.

He repaired Earth by starting first with a church, which was for Francis the new ark of the covenant, the dwelling place of God among us. A crumbling church yes, but also the earth upon which it rests and all creatures who dwell upon it and within it, and the seas whose waters Jesus himself calmed and from whose depths fishes of all sorts fed and nourished God's people and other creatures. Everything was from God, of God, and in

God, blessed and sustained in its existence. That is what needed renewing and rebuilding by listening to and heeding the words of the Gospel. The Gospel was for living, and to skew it otherwise was to betray Love who is Jesus Christ. Learning to love each person for the sake of the God who has come among us in the person of Jesus Christ is how the house of God is repaired. The fruit of this love of Christ is joy. The price of such love is grief over the betrayals, our own and that of others, of so great a love.

This incredible love is made real in Jesus Christ who is the Spouse of Francis's soul, a Lover so beautiful and good that he cannot even imagine letting himself be separated from this Christ. Not to return that infinite love is *the* sin. And Francis was determined to let nothing separate him from Christ Jesus; nothing will separate him from such love. He must have taken great consolation and hope from St. Paul's words:

> Who will separate us from the love of Christ? Will hardship, or distress, or persecution, or famine, or nakedness, or peril, or sword?... No, in all these things we are more than conquerors through him who loved us. For I am convinced that neither death, nor life, nor angels, nor rulers, nor things present, nor things to come, nor powers, nor height, nor depth, nor anything else in all creation, will be able to separate us from the love of God in Christ Jesus our Lord. (Romans 8:35; 37–39)

St. Francis's way was not to separate himself from all creation but to join Christ in his love for the creation of his hands. The revolution St. Francis became in his very person has its source in his intimate relationship with Christ Risen and present in all things through the Holy Spirit. Francis sees *in* Christ because he lives in Christ. Everything is redeemed and made holy in the Christ who lives in him and through whom he sees with the eyes of Christ, as it were. He needs no scientific facts to see what is happening to the world around us, the world we walk upon. He sees the wounded Christ in wounded Earth, in the wounded, broken person. This centrality of Christ is mystical and real, historical and transcendent, as well as imminent.

Then the other joy can flow freely, the joy we usually think of when we think of St. Francis, the joy that is play. It is best expressed in this quote by William Blake's biographer, Alexander Gilchrist. He says that Blake was "a divine child whose playthings were sun, moon, and stars, the heavens and the earth."[18]

This is the Francis who would pick up a stick from the ground and put it over his left arm. Then with his right arm he would draw across the stick a bow bent with a thread, as if he were playing the viol, singing about the Lord in French as he did so. This is the Francis whose songs of praise were sung in the vernacular, so that they could be understood and easily memorized, by everyone, educated and uneducated alike. This is the Francis who, the first time he went to Tuscany near Mount LaVerna and came upon the Castle of Montefeltro, saw at once that some sort of celebration was going on among the knights. He went up to the castle and saw that it was a banquet to celebrate the recent knighting of one of the Counts of Montefeltro. Seeing there were many nobles there, Francis said to Brother Leo, "Let's go in to the festival. With God's help we may reap a great spiritual harvest."

They entered the courtyard where the nobles were gathered and Francis leapt up on a low wall and began to preach, taking these words as his theme.

Tanto è il bene ch'io aspetto
Ch' ogni pene m'è diletto.
So great is the good I have in sight
That every pain brings me delight.[19]

This was a troubadour love-verse usually sung to the lady of the castle but that Francis proceeded to spiritualize and show how the love of God and human love are the same and only the object of that love differs. The scholar Rosalind Brooke writes that the romances and courtly love songs that Francis enjoyed and sang when he was a boy became for him songs and stories directed to God. Sometimes, as in this instance, he even played the role of God's Troubadour. He once said to a brother who had been a famous troubadour, "Brother Pacifico, when you preach, go and sing to the people 'The Canticle of the Creatures,'" saying, "We are God's minstrels, and as our fee for this performance, we want you to live in true penitence."[20]

Song and story and the spirit of playfulness inhabits and forms Franciscan wisdom and teaching. Story, especially, is itself a kind of playfulness, even when the story's message is somber or sad.

Stories are a way of knowing. Whether they record an actual happening, or are made up stories, they help us to know in a unique, individual case, the human condition in its simplicity and complexity, its striving and victories and defeats, and in its sorrows and joys. "What-If" stories, if true to reason and experience, tell us as much about someone or something as an actual reporting of the same. In fact, even an actual happening is already changed into a story when someone tells us what happened.

So, whether the story told actually happened or was made up, the story is its own truth and either works or not, depending on the skill, insight, and knowledge that the storyteller has or doesn't have.

We ask ourselves, Is this story believable? Would St. Francis have had this kind of exchange with Leo, for example, in the story of Perfect Joy? And does what St. Francis says sync with what we know of him from his own writings, and/or from other historical or hagiographical knowledge we have from sources closest to the time and milieu of the early friars?

As I began to retell this famous story of Perfect Joy using a modern English translation of *The Little Flowers of St. Francis,* I was aware that I had to be true to the basic truth of the story in *The Little Flowers of St. Francis.* The story has stood the test of time and can only only be tweaked from time to time for the contemporary ear.

This is the way a historical personage grows and resurrects, a revenant from the past, the original story remaining true to its first telling. The same holds for the stories told of the antics of St. Francis and the early brothers, the antics of "holy fools" who seem to us demented at times, perhaps because we have become too serious to allow ourselves to be "foolish" in the ways of God.

Humor and foolishness and playfulness in the Franciscan stories are possible because Francis and his early brothers had already experienced how conversion and turning one's life around is *the* foolishness in the eyes of those who don't have eyes to see or ears to hear. They gave up everything to follow in the footsteps of Christ. And so nothing else is that important, especially the hypocrisy of keeping up a false front to impress others or the energy it takes to inflate one's own self-importance. This is a foolishness that is true wisdom. As St. Paul said so dramatically in his first letter to the Corinthians:

> For the message of the cross is foolishness to those who are perishing, but to us who are being saved, it is the

power of God.... For God's foolishness is wiser than human wisdom, and God's weakness is stronger than human strength" (1 Corinthians 1:26–27).

And then in what is almost a portrait of the early Franciscans, St. Paul continues:

Consider your own call... not many of you were wise by human standards, not many were powerful, not many were of noble birth. But God chose what is foolish in the world to shame the wise; God chose what is weak to shame the strong; God chose what is low and despised in the world, things that are not, to reduce to nothing things that are, so that no one might boast in the presence of God (I Corinthians 1:28–30).

It is in this spirit that St. Francis was playful and foolish, why he played and why he played the fool. His vision is other. His is the vision of Hagia Sophia, Holy Wisdom, playing in the fields of the Lord. It is she who moved Francis to lick his lips when he said "Little Baby of Bethlehem," as if he were savoring the words. He would also say the word "Bethlehem," (*Bettleme* in Italian) making it sound like the bleating of a lamb. Sophia is why he would preach to the birds and they would not fly away but listen to him while they stretched out their necks and flapped their wings and gazed at him with their beaks open and would not fly away until he made the sign of the cross over them and dismissed them. Sophia is why when he dreamed of a little black hen with too many chicks to keep under her wing, he told his brothers, "I am that hen because I am small in stature and black and because I am to be simple as a dove and fly heavenward on wings of virtue."

Sophia is why he compared a friar to Sister Lark and said she had a hood like a friar and is a humble bird who goes in search of any grain, even in the garbage, and she sweetly praises God and reaches heavenward, even if her plumage is the color of the earth. It's why when a cicada jumped onto his finger, he began to stroke it with his other hand, saying, "Sing, Little Sister Cicada," and the cicada sang for a good hour as Francis harmonized by singing the praises of God. His Sophia is why when he came upon an almond tree and said, "Brother Almond, speak to me of God," the almond tree blossomed.

Sentimental stories? Or are they rather stories that flowed out of a radical upending of the usual expectations of the so-called "wise"? Are not these stories, and many more, really the result of a conversion that made of a leader among the revelers of Assisi a fool that mocks the self-importance of the leader and makes him laugh at himself, if he is wise enough to do so. These are stories of a completely unburdened and free soul who can even play with the animals and the fish and plants, a man who, as the Rumi translator, Coleman Barks, once said, had become so light the birds came and rested on his shoulders.

Sing, Francis, sing! Play in the fields of the Lord!

THE WISDOM OF ST. FRANCIS

St. Francis was sure that spiritual joy is the safest remedy against the thousand snares and wiles of the enemy. He used to say, "The devil is most happy when he can snatch from a servant of God true joy of spirit. He carries dust with him to throw into the smallest chinks of conscience and thus soil one's mental candor and purity of life. But if joy of spirit fills the heart, the serpent shoots his deadly venom in vain."

—Thomas of Celano, *Second Life of St. Francis*, 125

If at times temptation and despondency come along to try me, and I see joy in my companions, then I immediately recover and let go of the temptation or depression. The joy I admire in others restores my own inward and outward joy.

—*Mirror of Perfection*, 96

Since spiritual joy springs from the heart's innocence and the purity of incessant prayer, these are the two virtues we need to acquire and keep. Then that joy which I long to see and feel in myself and others, that inward joy, will be an edification to my neighbor and a reproach to the Enemy. For sadness is his and those who follow him; rejoicing and always being happy in the Lord is ours.

—*Mirror of Perfection*, 95

CHAPTER | *eight*

THE TEACHING OF TEACHINGS

Love

O grace abounding and allowing me to dare
to fix my gaze on the Eternal Light,
 so deep my vision was consumed by It!

I saw how it contains within its depths
 all things bound in a single book by love
of which creation is the scattered leaves:

....

And one is so transformed within that Light
 that it would be impossible to think
 of ever turning one's eyes from that sight,

because the good which is the goal of will
 is all collected there, and outside it
 all is defective that is perfect there.[21]

—Dante

LOVE IS THE TEACHING BEHIND ALL THE teachings of St. Francis. And it is St. Augustine who best summarizes "why" and "how" Francis, the son of Bernardone, became Francis, the son of God, Francis, the saint. In his *Confessions* St. Augustine writes:

> Late have I loved you, beauty so old and so new; late have I loved you. And see, you were within and I was in the external world and sought you there, and in my unlovely state I plunged into those lovely created things which you made. You were with me, and I was not with you. The lovely things kept me far from you, though if they did not have their existence in you, they had no existence at all.[22]

Was there a defining moment when Francis realized that it was God he was trying to love? And was it an experience like St. Augustine's in which he realized that God had been there all along loving him, though only now did he realize it?

It may have been when Francis heard the Lord's voice in Spoleto when he was on his way to Apulia to fight in the papal army there. Was it in this dream when he heard a voice saying:

"Francis, is it better to serve the Lord or the servant?"

"Why, the Lord, Sir."

"Then why are you serving the servant? Return to Assisi, and it will be shown you what you are to do."

And Francis returns home to Assisi, a seeming coward in flight from the battle.

Or was it when Francis went among lepers that he found God loving him in so unexpected a place among those who previously had repulsed him?

Or was it when he was wandering the countryside lost as to what he was to do with his life and heard the voice from the cross in the abandoned church of San Damiano, "Francis, go and repair my house which, as you see, is falling into ruins"?

Whenever and whatever happened, Francis fell in love with the love who is Infinite Love, a love that made him cry out: "May the fiery and honey-sweet power of your love, O Lord, wean me from all things under heaven, so that I may die for love of your love, who deigned to die for love of my love."[23]

Such a radical turnaround from a life of self-absorption to a life for the Other marked its public articulation when Francis was called before the Bishop of Assisi and assembled citizens to settle his differences with his father and return to Pietro Bernardone the money that was raised by Francis from the sale of a bolt of his father's cloth and one of his horses. At that point Francis had already given the money to the priest of San Damiano for the repair of the church, money the priest refused for fear of Bernardone. Francis, too, refused to take the money as his own but left it on the windowsill in the church.

So, was it when Francis placed whatever goods he had at his father's feet and then also stripped himself of the clothes he was wearing and stood there naked ready to follow the Christ who hung upon the cross stripped of his own garments? For it was then that Francis proclaimed to all those listening, "Up till now I have called Pietro Bernardone my father, but from now on I will say, "Our Father who art in Heaven." Was this the moment of Francis's realization that he belonged to God?

In the "Paradiso" of *The Divine Comedy* Dante reimagines this event as the moment of Francis's marriage to the Lady Poverty who had been Christ's spouse seven hundred years before, the only one who ascended the cross with Jesus. Of this Lady, Dante writes:

for even as a youth, he ran to war
against his father, on behalf of her –
the lady unto whom, just as to death,
none willingly unlocks the door; before
his spiritual court *et coram patre,*
he wed her; day by day he loved her more.[24]

The implication is that no one had been attracted to Lady Poverty, so unattractive was she, from the time Christ had embraced her on the cross until Francis appeared, a worthy knight to take her to himself, marrying the poor widowed bride of Christ. Dante turns to the tradition of medieval courtly love and spiritualizes it, Francis becoming in the process a spiritual knight of the Round Table of the Lord.

A very early Franciscan document, *Sacrum Commercium, The Sacred Exchange,* takes up this theme in the language of allegory. This precious text begins with words reminiscent of St. John of the Cross and the Bible's *Song of Songs:* "Francis began to go about in the streets and crossings of the city, relentlessly, like a persistent hunter, diligently seeking whom his heart loved. He inquired of those standing about, he questioned those who came near to him, saying, 'Have you seen her whom my heart loves?'"[25]

This kind of language and imagery for Franciscan poverty makes of poverty and penance a joyful enterprise, the joyful knight, Francis, going about the countryside as the embodiment of the good knight whose virtues are those of a knight of the new Round Table of the Lord. Poverty and penance, then, are not a grim affair, but the kind of derring-do a knight would perform to impress the Lady of the Castle, even rolling in briar bushes in the dead of winter to show his fidelity to her. This charges the tone of the early Franciscan Order with the chivalry and adventure of the Quest, a Spiritual Battle, fired by a deep and abiding love for Christ the Lord whose self-emptying is symbolized in Lady Poverty who was Christ's vesture.

And since Francis is already a poet and singer, he also becomes a medieval knight-troubadour who sings the praises of the God who sent him forth into the world, just as Jesus was sent forth from the Trinity to show the infinite love of God for God's creatures. One example of Francis the troubadour is his "Praises of God" that he sang in 1224, two years before his death while he was at La Verna, the holy mountain where he received the sacred stigmata of Christ.

Receiving the stigmata of Christ was an experience akin to a divine anointing of the good knight. The Lord whom he was late to love has now sealed Francis with his own wounds, a symbol of Francis's identification with the Poor Crucified Christ. It was on Mount La Verna that Francis was moved to sing the mantra-like song of the lover, a litany of love and praise:

> You are holy, Lord,
> God alone, You
> who work marvels.
> You are strong,
> You are grand.
> You are most high.
> You are the Almighty King,
> You, O Holy Father,
> King of heaven and earth.
> You are three and one,
> the Lord God of gods;
> You are the Good,

every good,
the highest good,
the Lord God, living and true.
You are love, charity.
You are wisdom.
You are humility.
You are patience.
You are beauty.
You are safety.
You are rest.
You are joy and gladness.
You are our hope.
You are our justice.
You are temperance.
You are all our treasure overflowing.
You are beauty.
You are meekness.
You are our protector.
You are our guardian and defender.
You are our strength.
You are refreshment.
You are our hope.
You are our faith.
You are our charity.
You are our total delight.
You are our eternal life,
great and wondrous Lord,
God All-Powerful,
merciful Savior!

In these "Praises of the Lord God Most High" are contained Francis's experience of God. This is who this God he has loved late and long has become for him. These praises say, "O God, this is your song, you who are beauty so old and new. Late have I loved you." And through it all Francis has tried to return such incredible love, a return of love that, Francis being Francis, was a great, though humble, love. As he sang at the end of his "Canticle of the Creatures," we are to praise God *"con grande umilitate,"* with grand humility, not a puny, wimpy humility but a paradoxically huge, grand humility. For all his littleness and humility, there was in Francis something big, a heart full of largeness and largesse.

Once Francis knew God's love, he knew, as well, what St. Augustine put so beautifully. "And you see, you were within, and I was in the external world and sought you there, and in my unlovely state I plunged into those lovely created things you have made." That is the meaning of conversion: you realize that all your loves and desires were really misdirected love; what you really desired was God, the God who has been there with you all the time, within you and in the lovely things God created that you mistook for God. You mistook the creature for the Creator, the very Creator who made them beautiful and in the Creator's own image.

And thus began Francis's long journey into God that at each step along the way was punctuated by learning again and again another truth that St. Augustine articulates at the beginning of his *Confessions*: "You have made us for You and our heart is restless until it finds its rest in You."[26]

It was a journey that involved learning to love anew the things of creation, his love constantly being purified by the overarching love of God. It was like a return to the Garden of Eden seeking again and again to restore the Paradise humans had so cavalierly destroyed. The journey forward into God is a journey backward to an original innocence we never fully recover but where a sort of semi-paradise happens when love turns into charity. This is the highest of all loves, which Christ defined as the love of God and the love of neighbor, the total love of God leading to true love of neighbor and the true love of neighbor leading to the love of God.

Love God and do as you will, says St. Augustine, for love is its own commandment. That is how St. Francis took it and lived it. He sinned, as all humans do, but after his conversion, he always knew when he had sinned because Love's commandment drew him back to the divine love that underpinned everything he was and did. It was not so much fear of punishment that motivated Francis but rather his commitment to him whom he loved, Jesus Christ. To separate oneself from Christ would be *the* sin for Francis. If he feared anything, it would have been that he would betray Christ, the love of his life. And Francis held fast to his commitment to Christ to the very end of his life.

Francis knew he was dying. A doctor friend from Arezzo had come to visit him and told him that with God's grace, all would be well. But Francis knew his friend was trying to make him feel better about his exhaustion and acute pain. So he said in return,
"Please tell me the truth. Whether I live or die makes no difference to me. I only want to do God's will."
"Well, then dear Brother Francis, as a doctor, I have to tell you that your illness is incurable, and as your friend, I need to say further that I believe you will die at the end of September or beginning of October."
Francis was ecstatic! He lifted his arms toward heaven and said, "Welcome, Sister Death."

And when that moment finally came in early October, Francis called to Brother Angelo and Brother Leo to come to where he lay on the ground and sing for him "The Canticle of the Creatures." Which they did, even as their voices broke with sobs. And when they came to the end, Francis, even in his weakness, sang a final verse he composed spontaneously.

Praise to you, my Lord, for our Sister bodily death,
from whom no living creature can escape.
How dreadful for those who die in sin.
How lovely for those she finds in
Your most holy will,
For the second death can do them no harm.

O praise and bless my Lord,
thank Him and serve Him
Humbly but grandly!

His own song defined love for him. It was to live and be in God's most holy will. And Francis has learned from Christ's own words in the Gospels what God's will is for those who love him. They are to feed the hungry, give drink to those who thirst, welcome the stranger, clothe the naked, visit the sick and those in prison. And they are to do all that for love of his love who did the same for us when he walked among us.

He remembered when he was hungry and thirsty, and a stranger, and naked, sick and in prison. And there were those who gave him food and water, and welcomed him and the brothers when they were on the road, and those who visited him when he was sick, and wanted to visit him in prison and could not.

Love is of the heart, Francis thought, but loving is about acting and living out God's will revealed in Jesus Christ and in those who love him. How simple it all was if you loved the Lord. And it was good, and now he had done what was his to do. He prayed the brothers would do now what was theirs to do.

And that is how Francis died. It was the evening of October 3, 1226, in the twentieth year of his conversion. After the brothers had laid their father, the cloth merchant's son, on ground covered with a coarse, threadbare cloth, he asked them to sprinkle him with dust and ashes. Then in a quiet but determined voice he, God's troubadour to the end, began to intone Psalm 142, and the brothers joined him in praying. Certain phrases brought a sudden light and joy to his eyes now dark with blindness, and he savored them and held them longer in his heart:

> With my voice I cry to the Lord;
> with my voice I make
> supplication to the Lord.
> ....
> I cry to you, O Lord;
> I say, "You are my refuge,
> my portion in the land of the living."
> Give heed to my cry,
> for I am brought very low.
> ....
> Bring me out of prison,
> so that I may give thanks to your name.
> The righteous will surround me,
> for you will deal bountifully with me.

And Jesus was there hearing him, calling him, delivering him from his final prison, and he was free at last to love him who was his heart's desire.

And when his soul began its beautiful flight, a flock of larks alighted on the hut where Francis's body lay no longer distorted with suffering and pain, but lightsome and handsome, looking like a young man in love, happily sleeping, dreaming of his beloved. And the larks began to sing.

The spirituality of St. Francis is not so much about the heroic deed as it is about the heroic love with which even the smallest deed is done. That is very clear from the quintessential story of Perfect Joy. It is not what Francis and Leo endure from the abusive brother that counts. It is, as Francis says to Leo, when we bear such abuse and suffering, "remembering the sufferings of Christ, the Blessed One, and how He taught us to bear all things for love of Him, then write down, Brother Leo, 'This is perfect joy.'"

Francis loved Christ and wanted to die into his love who is the incarnation of how far God will go in his love for us. He wants to be one with the Beloved, even in his rejection and suffering and unjust death at the hands of those for whom he came to reveal the goodness and love of God. It is only in the dimension of love that the marvelous dimension that the modern mystic Simone Weil speaks of, is saved from a kind of twisted masochism which overemphasizing the cross can become. She writes:

> Affliction is a marvel of divine technique. It is a simple and ingenious device which introduces into the soul of a finite creature the immensity of force, blind, brutal, and cold. The infinite distance separating God from the creature is entirely concentrated into one point to pierce the soul in its center…. In this marvelous dimension, the soul, without leaving the place and the instant where the body to which it is united is situated, can cross the

totality of space and time and come into the very presence of God.[27]

Affliction can do just the opposite and drive the soul into itself if there is not also love and a longing to know God. It is the mystery of the cross of Christ, namely not what Christ endured, but *why* he endured. Love was the reason, a love that was divine and, as such, not only endured those three hours on the cross, but did so out of love, a love that embraced all human suffering. It is Christ's surrender to the will of the Father that reveals the depth and breadth of Christ's love for the Father. And it is when we can say these words of Christ, "Father, into your hands I commend my spirit," that affliction becomes the marvelous dimension that brings us into the presence of God. For love is ultimately of the will, the will to do God's will being the ultimate act of love.

There is also the dimension of loving what is divine. Francis was in love with God. How, then, does he approach the Most Holy, the Divine? Even with love in one's heart, it is still God's presence the holy man or woman is seeking to enter. In one of his entries in *The Blue Octavo Notebooks*, Franz Kafka writes:

> Before setting foot in the Holy of Holies you must take off your shoes, yet not only your shoes, but everything; you must take off your travelling garments and lay down your luggage; and under that you must shed your nakedness and everything that hides beneath that, and then the core and the core of the core, then the remainder and then the residue and then even the glimmer of undying fire. Only the fire itself is absorbed by the Holy of Holies and lets itself be absorbed by it; neither can resist the other.[28]

Fire, of course, is one of *the* symbols of love, the heart enkindled with love. Love, love, love. That is the reason that saints do things that seem strange to us. That is why Francis sometimes seems to be excessive in his penances and fasting: his rolling in the snow or briar bushes, for example, to ward off temptations, or fasting for forty days, eating only a half loaf of bread and drinking minimal water the while, as Francis is said to have done one Lent on an island in Lake Trasimeno.

On another occasion he had made a little basket. And then when he went into prayer and kept thinking of the little basket instead of focusing on God, he went out and destroyed the basket. It seems such a violent thing to do. Was he thinking of Jesus's words, "The kingdom of heaven has suffered violence, and the violent take it by force" (Matthew 11:12)? Was he thinking he had not been strong enough to subdue his own ego? Or was it the fear that he'd been unfaithful to the Lord of prayer by not being fully present to God because of the basket's distraction? Or was it simply the need in Francis to be single-minded in his fidelity to his practice of being present to God? Whatever the reason, we do well not to try to mimic the saints in their eccentricities and even in their sometimes excessive practices, especially if they are of another time and place than ours with different sensibilities and ways of being good and Godlike people. We need to remember that saints are spiritual heroes with an enormous capacity for love.

Slavish imitation is not what holiness is about, but rather it's about learning to love God in our own time and place with its own sensibilities and ways of following in the footsteps of Jesus with all our heart and mind and soul. It's about doing and making choices commensurate with our own capacities, our own strength and/or weakness of mind and body. We don't have to be nutty to be a saint, but being in love with God will sometimes move us to do things that others will consider nutty or unbalanced.

In Francis's life, it was the *crucified* Savior who spoke to him from the cross of San Damiano and whom he saw in lepers. And it was the *crucified* Savior he first fell in love with. The suffering Jesus moved him to tears, and in pity and compassion he wanted to join Jesus in his suffering to show how much he loved him. And so he did "foolish" things at times to show his love, to keep focused and faithful to the Christ who revealed himself to a shopkeeper's son who longed to be a knight and ended up choosing instead to be a happy beggar who sang songs of love and lived and preached the Gospel of the love of God who was made real for him in the words and life of God's Son.

The human condition being what it is, love in the end involves a choice to love the Love that created and redeemed us, even in the face of affliction, abandonment, and death. "And that, Brother Leo, is perfect joy, a love purified by the love of God." That is the secret and perfect teaching of St. Francis of Assisi.

THE WISDOM OF ST. FRANCIS

I ask the sick that in everything you give thanks to the Creator. And whatever it might be that the Lord wants for you, whether it be health or sickness, let that be what you want also. For all those the Lord has 'destined for eternal life' (Acts 13: 49), he teaches by using the allurement of trials and sickness and compunction of spirit.

—Rule of 1221, Chapter X

Most High, Glorious God,
enlighten the darkness of my heart,
and give me correct faith,
sure hope and perfect charity,
with understanding and knowledge, Lord,
so that I may fulfill your holy and true command,
Amen.

—A Prayer before the Crucifix

O to have a Father in heaven, how glorious and holy and great that is! O to have a Spouse in heaven, how holy, beautiful, and lovable! O to have such a Brother, how holy and how beloved, how pleasing and lowly, peaceful and sweet and lovable and desirable above all things! And O to have such a Son, who laid down his life for his sheep and who prayed to the Father for us saying: 'Holy Father, keep those you have given me true to your name' (John 17:11).

—A Letter to All the Faithful

If you were so intelligent and wise that you had all knowledge and wisdom and you knew how to interpret all languages and could accurately divine heavenly things, in all this you could not glory.... Likewise, if you were more handsome and more rich than others, and also could work wonders, like driving out demons, all these things are only obstacles to you and none of them belongs to you, and in none of them can you glory. But in this we *can* glory: in our infirmities, in carrying every day the holy cross of our Lord Jesus Christ.

—Admonition 5

In eating and drinking, in sleeping and satisfying the other necessities of the body, you should take the measure of your own physical tolerance so that Brother Body doesn't rebel.

—*Mirror of Perfection,* 97

I exhort you to know your own constitution; for one of you might be able to get along on less food than another, and I wouldn't want you who may need more food to think you have to imitate someone who needs less. You each must know your own physical make-up and allow your body its needs, so that it has strength to serve the spirit. For just as we are bound to avoid overindulgence in food, which harms both body and soul, so we must also avoid exaggerated abstinence.

—*Mirror of Perfection,* 27

The Lord gave me such faith in churches that I used to simply pray these words: "We adore you, Lord Jesus Christ, in all your churches in the whole world, and we bless you because through your holy cross you have redeemed the world."

—*The Testament* of St. Francis

When you are visited by the Lord in prayer, you should say, "Lord, you have sent me this comfort from heaven, even though I am a sinner and unworthy, and I entrust it to your keeping because I feel like a thief of your treasures." And when you leave your prayer, you should seem to be only a poor little sinner, and not someone especially graced by God.

—St. Francis in St. Bonaventure's
Major Life of St. Francis

Let us bless the Lord God,
living and true;
let us always offer him
praise and glory,
honor and blessing,
and refer every good to him.
Amen. Amen. So be it. So be it.

—Office of the Passion

Let us love the Lord God with all our heart and all our
soul, with all our mind and all our strength and with
fortitude and with total understanding, with all of our
power, with every effort, every affection, every emotion,
every desire, and every wish.

—Rule of 1221, Chapter XXIII

God alone is kind
innocent
pure
from whom and through whom and in whom is
all pardon
all grace
all glory
of all the penitent and the just
of all the blessed who rejoice together in
heaven.

—Rule of 1221, Chapter XXIII

Let us all
wherever we are
in every place
at every hour

at every time of day
every day and continually
believe truly and humbly.

—Rule of 1221, Chapter XXIII

Let us desire nothing else
let us wish for nothing else
let nothing else please us
and cause us delight
except our Creator and Redeemer and Savior,
the one true God.

—Rule of 1221, Chapter XXIII

God is the fullness of Good
all good, every good, the true and supreme good.
He alone is good
merciful and gentle
delectable and sweet.
He alone is holy
just and true
holy and right.

—Rule of 1221, Chapter XXIII

A Chronology

1182: St. Francis is born in Assisi to Pietro Bernardone and Lady Pica.

1193: St. Clare is born in Assisi to Favarone and Ortolana of the House of Offreduccio.

1198: The citizens of Assisi destroy the Rocca Maggiore, the fortress that towered above the city, a symbol of imperial sovereignty.

1199-1200: Civil war in Assisi results in the establishment of a commune.

1202 (November): Perugia and Assisi are at war. Assisi is defeated at Ponte San Giovanni near the town of Collestrada. Francis is a prisoner of war for a year in Perugia.

1203-1204: Francis is freed and returns to Assisi. He suffers a long illness at home in Assisi during 1204.

1205 (spring): Francis decides to join the Papal Army in Apulia, south of Rome. He journeys only as far as neighboring Spoleto where he is told in a dream to return to Assisi.

1205 (fall): The San Damiano crucifix speaks to Francis: "Go and repair my house which, as you see, is falling into ruin." Francis takes some of his father's cloth to Foligno and sells it. He gives the money to the priest of San Damiano, who refuses it out of fear of Francis's father.

1206 (early): Francis's father takes him before the bishop's court for the return of his money; Francis returns his possessions, including his clothing and renounces his father before the bishop and assembled citizens, then leaves for Gubbio, where he visits a friend and nurses lepers.

1206 (summer and fall): Francis returns to Assisi dressed as a hermit and begins to repair the church of San Damiano.

1206 – 1208 (February): Francis restores San Damiano, the small chapel of San Pietro (which is no longer standing), and the Porziuncola (St. Mary of the Angels).

1208 (February 24): At the Porziuncola Francis hears the Gospel for the Feast of St. Matthias and embraces Gospel poverty. He changes his leather belt for a rope cincture. He begins to preach.

1208 (April 16): Bernard of Quintavalle and Peter Catanii join Francis. On April 23rd Giles joins them.

1208 (summer): Three more brothers join.

1209 (spring): The number of Francis's companions grows to eleven. Francis writes a short Rule, and they journey to Rome where Pope Innocent III verbally approves Francis's Rule. The brothers settle at Rivotorto on their return to Assisi.

1209 or 1210: The brothers move to the church of St. Mary of the Angels near Rivo Torto on the plain below Assisi. Francis calls the church, "Porziuncola," Little Portion.

1211: Francis plans to go to Syria, but high winds ruin his plans.

1212 (March 18 or 19): St. Clare, the first Franciscan woman, is received into the Order at the Porziuncola. She goes first to the Benedictine Monastery of San Paolo delle Abbadesse in Bastia, and five days later Clare moves to Sant' Angelo in Panzo, the home of a group of penitent women near Assisi. Several weeks later Bishop Guido of Assisi provides the church of San Damiano as a monastery for Clare and her companions, including her sister Agnes, who has since joined them.

1215 (November): Francis is in Rome during the Fourth Lateran Council. He meets St. Dominic.

1213-15: The missionary journeys of the brothers. Francis goes to Spain.

1216 (July 16): Pope Innocent III dies. Honorius III succeeds.

1216 (summer): The Porziuncola Plenary Indulgence (Il Perdono, the Pardon) granted by Honorius III.

1217 (May 5): At the General Chapter at the Porziuncola, the first missionary brothers are sent forth to cross the Alps and the Mediterranean.

1219 (May): The First Franciscan Martyrs leave for Morocco. Francis sails for Damietta in Egypt.

1219 (fall): Francis is given access to the Sultan, Malik-al-Kamil, for over twenty days. The two become friends.

1220: Francis returns to Italy and resigns as minister general of the order. Peter Catanii is chosen to replace him.

1221: Peter Catanii dies; Brother Elias is named vicar general.

1221: Rule of the Third Order Secular Franciscans is approved by Pope Honorius III.

1223 (November 29): Honorius III approves the Rule of St. Francis.

1223 (Christmas): Francis celebrates Christmas at Greccio with a live crèche.

1224 (August 12-September 29) Francis, fasting in preparation for the Feast of St. Michael the Archangel on September 29, receives the sacred stigmata around September 14, the Feast of the Holy Cross.

1225 (early): Francis returns to Assisi and stays in a hut, which St. Clare has had built for him next to the Monastery of San Damiano.

1225 (March - May): Francis composes "The Canticle of the Creatures" at San Damiano. His eye disease worsens.

1225 (July): Urged by Brother Elias and Cardinal Hugolino (future Gregory IX), Francis goes to Fonte Colombo near Rieti to have his eyes cauterized.

1225: Francis adds a stanza to "The Canticle of the Creatures" on pardon and peace and asks one of the brothers to sing the revised canticle to the feuding Bishop and Mayor of Assisi. The two men are reconciled.

1226 (August-early September): Francis is taken to the bishop's palace in Assisi, his health failing.

1226 (September): Realizing he will die soon, Francis insists on being carried to the Porziuncola. He blesses Assisi as he departs the city.

1226 (October 3): Francis dies at the Porziuncola. He is buried the next day in San Giorgio in Assisi, where today the Basilica of St. Clare has replaced the Church of San Giorgio.

1227 (March 19): Cardinal Ugolino is elected pope, taking the name, Gregory IX.

1228 (July 16): Gregory IX canonizes St. Francis.

1230 (May 25): The body of St. Francis is transferred from San Giorgio to the new basilica constructed in his honor.

1253 (August 11): St. Clare dies at San Damiano and is buried in the Church of San Giorgio where the body of St. Francis was first buried.

1255 (August 12): Alexander IV canonizes St. Clare at Anagni, south of Rome.

APPENDIX II

A Brief Life of Saint Francis

He is born in 1182 in the Umbrian town of Assisi and is baptized, John. At the time of his baptism his father is away on a business trip to France; and when he returns, he changes his son's name to Francesco, the Frenchman.

True to his name, the boy grows up enamored of the French language and of the tales of the knights and ladies of French romance. He is a carefree, generous young man who pursues the good life with gusto, partying and carousing with his friends. But throughout all the levity of his younger years, he dreams of becoming a knight, a serious, bloody enterprise. And when a war breaks out between Assisi and its neighbor, Perugia, he gets his chance to ride off to war in hopes that his valor will earn him knighthood. Instead, the Assisi troops are defeated in the very first skirmish, and Francis is captured and made a prisoner of war in Perugia.

How could he have known that this was the end of war for him, this humiliating defeat of his hometown? And how could he have known that the year of imprisonment in a Perugian prison would change him so deeply? At just twenty-one years old, Francis returns home to Assisi a broken man, to lie in bed for a year. The richest young man in Assisi, Francis spends a year in prison, then a year in bed. His companions had dubbed him the King of the Revels: Francis, the son of the cloth merchant

Pietro Bernardone and the French woman Lady Pica. And now there are no revels for him. Instead he is imprisoned by the effects of his experience in battle, a battle that leaves him broken, both physically and psychologically.

When he begins to heal, he thinks his cure will come by conquering his fear and getting back on his war horse. He decides to go to war again as a knight in the papal army battling the forces of the Holy Roman Emperor, but God has other plans. In a vision, God tells Francis to return to Assisi where it will be revealed to him what he is to do. And so Francis retreats from war, returning home once again, this time looking like a coward who has deserted even before he gets to the battle itself. He roams the countryside feeling lost and abandoned; he visits abandoned churches. Then one day while he is praying before the crucifix of the dilapidated little chapel of San Damiano outside the walls of Assisi, he receives his call from God. From the crucifix comes the voice once again, "Francis, go and repair my house which, as you see, is falling into ruin."

Francis is to build and to repair, not to tear down with weapons of destruction. He begins to beg stones and repairs with his own hands the run-down chapel of San Damiano, which is the "house" Francis believes his vision refers to. It is this house, this little church, but it is more. It is the larger house, the Church of Christ itself that he is to repair.

Francis learns this larger implication of the vision one day when he sees a leper on the road and impulsively jumps from his horse, gives coins to the leper, and embraces him. Unbelievably, he is not repulsed but filled with joy, for he realizes he has embraced his Lord, Jesus Christ.

And so it happens that Francis goes to live among the lepers, ministering to them and learning from them. Here, he realizes, are the living stones; and together, they are building the kingdom of God on earth. Here is God among the rejected, the despised, the poor.

Thus it begins, the Franciscan rebuilding of the Church. Others soon join Francis, and they become a brotherhood, and the Church approves their way of life to live with the poor as poor men who observe the Holy Gospel wholeheartedly.

Francis and the brothers preach and work with their hands for their daily bread; and when they receive nothing for their labor, they beg for food. They continue to live with the lepers, making mercy with them and making peace with them and with all people and all creation by making peace with their own aversion to the lepers. They embrace them, instead of running away.

Women come to join them; the first is Clare, the daughter of the knight Favarone di Offreduccio. And the Bishop of Assisi gives Clare and her companions, as their cloister, the once abandoned church of San Damiano, the church Francis himself restored with his own hands at Christ's command. There they live in extreme Gospel poverty in contemplation of the Poor Crucified Christ. They work with their hands and depend on the begging of the brothers for their sustenance. They pray for and minister to the sick who are brought to their door.

Francis, in the meantime, is expanding the brothers' ministry beyond Assisi to all of Italy and beyond. He himself, with one or two brothers, makes missionary journeys preaching conversion and forgiveness which he sees as *the* means of peacemaking. He travels to Spain, France, Switzerland, Dalmatia, and even to Syria, the Holy Land, and Egypt during the Fifth Crusade. He tries to be a peacemaker between the Christians and Muslims, going so far as to enter the camp of the sultan, again preaching conversion of heart and forgiveness. The sultan listens and gives Francis safe passage through his kingdom.

The animal and plant worlds, too, receive Francis's compassionate love. He reaches out to and reveres all created things.

He preaches to the animals and birds and fish. He embraces and tames the ravenous wolf of Gubbio.

He preaches always the God-man, Jesus Christ. Francis tries to make him visible and tangible, as when, three years before his death, he celebrates Midnight Mass with live animals to recreate the first Christmas, thus popularizing the tradition of the Christmas crib.

The following year, while Francis is in deep prayer on the mountain of La Verna in Tuscany, he receives the sacred stigmata, the five wounds of Christ, becoming himself a visible image of his crucified Lord.

He then returns to Assisi, to the church of San Damiano where Clare and her sisters have a small lean-to built for him next to the church where Christ spoke to him from the crucifix. Two months later he sings his "Canticle of the Creatures," his swan song that sums up his life and attests to the peace, joy, and integration a life of love and forgiveness brings. He sings of all creatures as his brothers and sisters and bids them forgive one another if they want to be crowned by God. He then welcomes even death as his sister and embraces her. He is forty-four years old. It is the year 1226.

The man who longed to be a knight, a man of war, dies a man of peace, at peace with God, with himself, and with all of creation. God had changed his heart, and his changed heart changes the world.

NOTES

1. Murray Bodo, *A Far Country Near: Poems new and Selected*, (Phoenix: Tau, 2018), 280.
2. Bonaventure, *The Life of St. Francis*, trans. Ewert Cousins. (New York: Paulist, 1978), 194.
3. Author's translation in *Through the Year with Francis of Assisi*, 82.
4. *The Legend of Perugia 114, Omnibus*, 1088.
5. Brother Thomas of Celano, *The Life of St. Francis of Assisi* and *The Treatise of Miracles*, trans. by Catherine Bolton, (Assisi: Editrice Minerva, 2004), Chapter XXX, 80.
6. Thomas of Celano, *The First Life of St. Francis*, 91, author's translation.
7. "Message of His Holiness Pope Francis for World Communications Day" given on 24 January 2018, Libreria Editrice Vaticana.
8. A Pope Francis Lexicon, edited by Cindy Wooden and Joshua J. McElwee (Collegeville, Minnesota: Liturgical Press, 2017), 179.
9. William Blake, "London," Songs of Innocence and Experience, in The Poems of William Blake (London: Oxford University Press, 1960), 102.
10. Blake, 85.
11. Thomas of Celano, *Second Life*, 165, author's translation.
12. Thomas of Celano, *First Life of St. Francis*, 80-81.
13. *Poems of Gerard Manley Hopkins* (New York and London: Oxford University Press, 1948), 70
14. John Duns Scotus, *Parisiensia, III, vii, 4*.
15. Ignazio Silone, *Bread and Wine* in *The Abruzzo Trilogy*. (Hanover, New Hampshire: Zoland Books, 2000), 461.
16. Omnibus, p. 1503.

17. Murray Bodo, *Francis: The Journey and theDream,* (Cincinnati: St. Anthony Messenger Press, 1988), 51

18. Alexander Gilchrist, *The Life of William Blake* (Mineola, NY: Dover Publications, 2017), 3.

19. Arnoldo Fortini, *Francis of Assisi,* (New York: Crossroad, 1981), 550.

20. Rosalind Brooke, *The Image of St. Francis: Responses to Sainthood in the Thirteenth Century,* (Cambridge: Cambridge University Press, 2006), 15-16.

21. *The Portable Dante,* trans, edited by Mark Musa, (New York: Penguin Books, 1995), *The Divine Comedy,* "Paradise," Canto XXIII, lines 82-87; 100-105, 583.

22. Augustine, *Confessions,* trans. Henry Chadwick, Oxford's World's Classics, (Oxford, 199_), 10.38, 201.

23. Attributed to St. Francis by St. Bernardine of Siena and Ubertino da Casale.

24. Allen Mandelbaum, *The Divine Comedy of Dante Alighieri: Paradiso XI: 58-63* (Berkeley: University of California Press, 1984).

25. Omnibus, 1553

26. Augustine, *Confessions: Books I – IV,* edited by Gillian Clark, (Cambridge: Cambridge University Press, 1995), 29

27. Simone Weil, *Waiting for God,* Emma Craufurd trans. (New York: Harper Collins, 2001) 81.

28. Franz Kafka, *The Blue Octavo Notebooks,* ed. Max Brod, (Cambridge: MA: Exact Change, 1991), 39.

ABOUT THE AUTHOR

Murray Bodo, OFM, is a Franciscan priest, a member of the Franciscan Academy and an award-winning author of many books, including *Francis: The Journey and the Dream, Francis and Jesus,* and *Enter Assisi.* As an internationally known poet, Fr. Bodo has participated in poetry readings in Europe and the United States. He lives in Cincinnati, Ohio, and travels yearly to Rome and Assisi, Italy, where he leads Franciscan pilgrimages.